all that grows

CLARA OBLIGADO

all that grows

nature and writing

Translated from the Spanish by Fiona Mackintosh

CONTENTS

FOREWORD
NICOLE HERVÁS IBAÑEZ

"I jot down in my notebook: to write is to take root in the air."

When I first read *all that grows*, recommended by a friend, I knew that it was one of those books that I would always keep close and which must be shared. I knew that just as it arrived in my hands, it had to reach many more. That is how I came to give it to Alexandra Grant, X Artists' Books' publisher. She agreed that it should be translated into English, so that the book could continue its journey and Clara Obligado's words could keep taking root in other airs and being read under other skies.

Clara's writing is as direct and bold as it is poetic and nurturing. Though personal and forged from her distinct experiences, the images, ideas and sensations that live in her text makes us feel that we, her readers, share a world view. Clara's words create a constellation in which other authors, readers and activists might find a home, a place to shape *all that grows*.

One need not have been raised in the pampa nor have lived in exile to see oneself reflected in Clara's metaphors, her trees, or her memory. Her reflective capacity, her spirit of transformation, and above all, her ode to life, give me a sense of hope—that through creative expression our resilience expands.

Some of us grow up watching the *Tres Marías*. Others, The Great Bear. Whether seen from the north or the south, it doesn't matter what images the stars draw for us; what matters is the fact that we all observe them, that the constellations are part of our shared imaginary, no matter how they are named or what we see in them. During our work together, Clara said something that often comes back to mind: that we must never lose our enthusiasm. The enthusiasm to create, to observe, to discover. The enthusiasm for continuity and also for change. The enthusiasm to read a new book, to learn an unknown word, to feel a connection. The enthusiasm to live and go on living, even after tragedy. That silent force that keeps us moving forward. Because despite everything, life goes on; with or without our enthusiasm and it's up to us to choose how we move through this world.

Our childhood recollections take root in our memories. A geranium, our first love, or the singing of the cicadas constitute the foundations of our consciousness. Good, bad, sad, or transcendental, memories stay with us even if we move from our childhood landscape or change our point of view. Clara makes it clear that there is always space for the new, although it may be difficult to adopt a new vocabulary and call a *palta* an *aguagate*. In this book, Clara shows us how she accepted that the moon grows the other way around if we change hemispheres, and that there is always space for other songs and other trees to take root in our imaginations.

As the fifth publication in the X Artists' Books X Topics series, we aim to expand the reach of Clara's words and ideas, sowing them among new readers and strengthening the invisible bond between writing, nature and existence. We hope you enjoy this journey across hemispheres, dialects, and species as much as we did.

INTRODUCTION

*THE ROOT BOOK: CLARA OBLIGADO'S LITER**N**ATURE*

BY ERICA DURANTE

Rare are the books that defy gravity like an inverted hourglass yet maintain structural integrity. Clara Obligado's *all that grows: nature and writing* is one such book. Divided by an imaginary equatorial line, this essay unfurls into two hemispheres, with the austral taking the prominence. It is a tapestry of autobiography, bildungsroman, family album, and intimate atlas. Sotto voce, Obligado delivers a poignant reflection on exile and loss: an elegy for an unnamed love, and many others like him, who endured torture and disappearance during the Argentinian military dictatorship. Weaving marginalia from her personal library together with thoughts from her notebooks, Obligado guides us through landscapes as biodiverse as the pampa and the countryside of southwestern Spain. In a movement akin to a gentle breeze, her writing cradles us from shore to shore, without turbulence: a soft swing that carries us like seeds migrating through the air fluidly.

We step into this book as if crossing the threshold of an enchanted interspecies landscape, where all living organisms—from beneath the water to above the soil, from microscopic, like fungi, to massive, like holm oaks—are interconnected in an original symbiosis. Families of words and languages inhabit this protected ecosystem: they share roots that have branched into multiple arborescences, where etymologies nurture contemporary meanings. The act of writing is an intrinsic part of this landscape's ecosystem. It is not only biologically embedded in the venation of leaves and the cellulose fiber of barks—which will ultimately transform into paper, "everlasting words," and books—it also entails the same patient gestures that have tethered us to the soil since the Neolithic Revolution. Comparing words to seeds and bulbs, recycled texts to compost, and writers to those who plow, plant, fertilize, irrigate, prune, harvest, and tirelessly repeat this cycle is far from mere metaphor for Obligado. She likens herself to an epiphyte, whose roots are not attached to the ground but are aerial and grow upon another supporting plant. This identification as a living part of the vegetal world shows how vital and self-defining nature is to her understanding of our existence in the world.

Uprooted, transplanted, acclimated, flourishing, grafted, fertilized: these words help form the nuanced semantics that Obligado borrows from nature writing. Nature displays the most striking examples of survival, resilience, coexistence, diversity, and sustainability. In Obligado's animistic imagination, nature operates as a magnifying lens to reveal how phenomena that, from our anthropocentric perspective, we perceive as predominantly human, are inherent to the evolution of other species. Migration, for instance, is described as a biological and ecological pattern: centennial trees embark on migratory journeys without ever uprooting themselves from the soil; their seeds traverse great distances through winds and seas, germinating in faraway lands. Likewise, the names of fruits such as tomatoes and avocados reveal their passage from the Americas to European dinner tables. Within Obligado's cosmology, human displacement is one strand of an interdependent and cross-pollinated narrative of the natural world. Birds, insects, fish, and seeds share in the experience of exile, mirroring Obligado's own. Like resilient plants anchoring themselves to rocky cliffs, enduring storms and gusts, those compelled to expatriate—

be they exiles or refugees—must adapt amidst absence and nostalgia, grappling with a permanent sense of displacement and the daunting task of taking root beneath unfamiliar skies and within inhospitable soil. Losing the barycenter requires seeking balance at the margins; this is the essence of Obligado's oeuvre—disorienting, uncomfortable, and eccentric—because it distances itself from the centers of power and undermines the monolithic and nationalistic notion of a singular identity.

Obligado's essay invites readers on a contemplative promenade through a web of gardens. With each turn of a page, the mind is stirred and travels from one meditation to the next, along a synesthetic path where thoughts bloom with every step. Each element finds its rightful place in this literary landscape, echoing the perfect arrangement of a Japanese garden. Every fragment resonates harmoniously with the others, while ellipses serve as bridges, connecting the dots along Obligado's narrative pathway. Page after page, we find our place within a symbiotic ecosystem. Yet, as the book unfolds, we reluctantly acknowledge the departure from this insulated terrarium of thought in which Obligado has enveloped us. Within its transparent and sealed confines—reminiscent of both a globe and the bulb of an hourglass—she has transplanted us into an ideal environment where all things grow in a flawless blending of nature and writing.

If only one were an Indian, ready right away, and on the running horse, aslant in the air, briefly shaking again and again over the shaking ground, until one dropped the spurs for there were no spurs, until one cast off the reins for there were no reins, and one could hardly see the land ahead as a smoothly cropped heath, now without the horse's neck and head.

Franz Kafka, "Wish to Become an Indian"
translated by Mark Harman

south

There is an origin.

I'm sitting on a terrace. The white-painted chair creaks. In the corner, a flowerpot, *un tiesto*, that back then I call *una maceta*. I see it almost in a different dimension. It's a geranium, *un geranio*, or *malvón* as they would say in my land.

I see this spindly *malvón/geranio*, its little leaves dusty and rough. I see the way children see: for the first time.

An ellipsis. The night and its terrors, sleepless ghosts, rain lashing on the checkered terrace. By morning, the sun is pinned to a harmless sky. The flowerpot exudes humidity and the geranium wakes up and dances, stretching its little green arms; in the center a red flower has opened. I'm five years old and witnessing a miracle. I'm an Eve discovering the world, the passage of time, beauty, fragility.

That geranium will go on growing in my memory.

The ardent intensity of childhood senses, that obsessive gaze that discovers leaf veins, insect legs, scents. Before the birth of words there is touch, smell, hearing. Powder on butterfly wings, unfurling antennae, the perverse gaze of a grasshopper, the downward corkscrew of a eucalyptus leaf. On the gnarled trunk insects criss-cross their infinite stories. The smell of summer.

We remember before being able to name. There is a world of the senses that predates words, logic, time; we go back there, we dream it's ours again. A garden before time, an Eden that safeguards nostalgia, which we seek out when we're lost.

"Let us enter farther into the thicket."[1] In that original verdure we fuse with all that grows, we're part of the cosmos. "Part of," not arrogant individuals facing one another alone.

1 | Saint John of the Cross, "Spiritual Canticle," trans. E. Allison Peers.

I read María Zambrano.

Once I'm a writer, I will spend hours trying to pin down those emotions that precede language. To write, I muse while walking, is to head toward dreams, to imagine backwards.

Decades have gone by since that founding moment and only emotions are left in my memory. Are they part of me or outside me? A flower and a moment.

I will go on growing like that plant and I still have within me a deep-rooted joy in nature.

Emily Dickinson was—besides being a poet—a botanist, whose herbarium contains 424 species of wildflowers, organized according to Linnaeus's classification. I imagine the poet concentrating; she is barely fourteen years old and we are in the year 1845, in rural Massachusetts. In Dickinson's elegant calligraphy, the plant names are written in Latin; the herbarium begins with a common white jasmine and ends with a sprig of blue rosemary. Such simplicity.

To make a prairie it takes a clover and one bee,
One clover, and a bee,
And revery.
The revery alone will do,
If bees are few.

But there is also terror. Panicked animals fleeing in a storm, an erupting volcano. Decades later, almost in another life, I will peer down into a volcano in Nicaragua, into its monstrous power, its incandescent mouth that spews fire. In Guatemala a village was submerged under a highway of lava. After the disaster, I will see women sweeping up the never-ending ashes. Rings of fire, beauty, and horror. Writing also stems from the impulse to flee. Although I barely perceive my own tiny life, the mystery of nighttimes overcomes me. We're born in fear; hyenas tumble into the world bathed in testosterone, as soon as they hit the ground they must flee. To devour or be devoured.

In the countryside the world is an unbridled horizon. A dog barks. As if in echo, other dogs answer. The coded messages of animals, their invisible telegraphy, signs of danger or friendship. Species memory, inherited fear of the dark, bodies remembering ancestral lessons, life distilled over millions of years, a protective terror. In the sonorous undergrowth, night is split open by groans; I hide under the sheets. The dogs stop barking as abruptly as they started.

As the storm gets closer, the dog lies on its back, the dragonflies or *libélulas*, that are still called *alguaciles*, fly low. So many mysteries. To read nature as if it were a book, if only we could.

To read ourselves.

"Panic" comes from Greek, and refers to the god Pan, who overcame the enemies that terrified him by making a tremendous din. *Pan* refers to the god, and *oikos* to "house." So panic is the fear provoked by the house where this god lived.

"Crepúsculo," twilight, means "little death."

In the too-vast night I often suffer from insomnia, lose myself in bed; I turn, crawl, don't know where the walls are, get strangled by sheets and pillowcases.

My sister doesn't breathe; she shifts about and talks to herself, watches me with her vacant eyes, gives a mocking little giggle. She's tormented by the inhabitants of her dreams, she argues with them in an incomprehensible language. I try to sneak into her nightmares, but she doesn't let me.

Sometimes I jerk awake and she's there beside me, silently, in her nightdress. There but not there. If I put my feet down onto the floor someone will grab me by the ankles, if I get out of bed I won't be able to get back in; that primal fear links me to a chain of trembling beings. I shape the vertigo of night, the unbounded landscape, death, and nothingness. Nature and its terrifying indifference. I will stop being alone once I learn to read, I'll make myself a den under the sheets and shine a flashlight on the secret pages. If my mother finds me there'll be trouble; at home she enforces her martial law. We're isolated in the middle of the countryside and the lights cut out at eleven o'clock at night. I hunker down, think tactically, learn to survive. When the sky turns to turquoise, the cockcrows resound.

We die every day, at twilight.

However, sleep proves to us that we're not alone. When the sun hides itself, we rest as a herd, keeping each other warm. Cicadas, birds, frogs in the lake, all fall silent. We sleep and are awake in synchrony. All living beings know when it's nightfall.

From a very young age I go wandering off; I learn to steep myself in solitude as if it were liberated territory, unconstrained by parents, siblings, rules, and punishments. Alone, I'm free. Feet on the ground, head in the sky, where the birds live out their daily round. Standing stiffly on a post, a bird of prey sizes me up. I go walking by myself when no one's bothering about me. I flee and forage, I feel and fantasize, I go with the flow. I recognize, connect. The landscape moves through me, merges with my feelings, becomes a story: introduction, intrigue, denouement. Like fairy tale heroes: set off, journey and arrive, conquer a kingdom. The garden around the house. The park around the garden. Around the park, the orchard. In ever-increasing circles, the limitless pampa. And beyond that?

I read the world with my feet.

At lunchtime a bell rings and I'm first to appear; respecting certain rules keeps me invisible.

The ancient Romans read their future in the flight of birds, they'd cut them open lengthways and consult their organs for what would happen the next day; the word *avis*, bird, is hidden in the etymology of many words linked to divination.

"Auspicious," from *avis spicio*, I observe the birds.

"Augury," a priest who foretells destiny through the flight of birds.

"Haruspex," one capable of deciphering confused speech through inspecting entrails.

"Proclivous," *pro clivia avis*, of a bird of evil omen.

Though we may not be aware of it, words betray our history.

There's more sky than land in the pampa, the landscape wheels over my head. Summer evening falls and I walk to a point from which you can see the twilight. The southern sun lingers, there's still a while before it reaches the best bit of the day. Where does it go? The sky embraces the horizon with one blue and one red line. Beneath the first few stars, the night becomes peopled by lives that persist in darkness. A solitary bird sings, an animal whines. In the mysterious shadows, I too fade away.

Naked and happy, in the beginning we survived as part

and parcel of nature, in Eden, that was also called Paradise. An enclosed garden where no farming was done, where nothing alludes to the hard graft of plowing.

The Bible translates the Hebrew word "garden" (*gan*) with the Greek word *parádeisos*, which in turn comes from the Persian *pardês*, orchard, park, garden. It does not refer to untamed nature, God was systematic like a bookkeeper.

That is our founding story; in it we were subordinated to a god, and nature was subordinated to us. His finger points at us and we are turned into shepherds and gardeners.

There was an Eden, a vague territory where idealized ecology was cultivated. The image we have comes from Northern European painters, where an Adam and Eve looking like Dutch peasants, pale and red-haired, naked as frogs, are chatting by a tree. Were they really apples? According to tradition, there were no apples in paradise, but they were planted there by a translation error; *malus* can mean both "apple" and "evil." The fantasy of bountiful nature. Original mix-up. Reality and fiction. Evil and apples.

"Live in nature." "What nature gives us," understood as fleeing the "world." "Rustic" houses with oversized windows that give no protection from cold or heat, orchards and gardens. Flowers painted with the precision of a miniaturist. But life in the countryside is hours staring at the sky, drought, floods, hail. Poverty and work.

"The Garden of Eden," "Eden, the garden of God," "the garden of Jehovah," where trees beautify the landscape and provide sustenance. A perfect climate in which we could stroll naked and that can only be seen with a backward glance.

Were bygone days always better? Hence the primordial garden that inhabits desire or memory. Is that the source of the idea that every childhood has been a happy one, and that to grow up is to lose everything? As [Borges] said, "there are no paradises other than lost paradises."[2] What a sad assertion. I imagine Yahweh separating us from the trees of good and evil. Expelling us from the garden. Splitting us apart. Fumigating us.

The first punishment was botanical.

Scorching *siestas*, cicadas sawing the air, children's never-ending boredom. The adults evaporate and we are under strict orders not to go out. I'm one of five siblings, I sleep next to the youngest; she and I don't talk, it will take us until we're grown up to understand how much we love each other. I escape, spurred on by that drive that will accompany me throughout my life, running away from places where I don't want to be, never staying in places I can't run from. Getting away from home.

I cycle along dirt tracks to go see Jorge.

The air buzzes with gnats that get tangled in my hair; there are industrious bees, strolling ants, black beetles who waylay me with their rainbow reflections, they write secret signs in the dust, basking in the sun.

There are no trees in the pampa. If you plant them, they'll grow—the ground is fertile—but there is such a dense layer of vegetation that it stops the seeds from reaching the soil. On the endless plain, groups of trees around houses are called *montes*. When they begin being planted, this catalyzes the transformation of the landscape; large houses aping European buildings, formal parks with ornamental lakes and parterres, statues, bridges, avenues of poplars. "Picturesque" gardens, worth turning into a painting.

Jorge is a bit older than me. I'm the daughter of the local

2 | Jorge Luis Borges, "Posesión del ayer" [Possession of Yesterday], excerpt trans. Fiona Mackintosh.

rich man, he's the son of a farming couple. He was born in the Italian colony that branches out like a flowered stem of hard-worked plots of land. Our pieces of land are separated by a dirt track, but not only by that. His father is a tall Italian, paper-thin, gaunt, and taciturn, who nearly always wears work clothes two sizes too big, meticulously ironed. His mother is a no-nonsense *criolla* who talks at the top of her voice and plants geraniums, stonecrops, and cactuses: succulents like her who don't need much looking after. In one corner, where the humidity makes things coil up, the curly hair of a fern waits for a gust of wind to release its spores. Pubescent plant hairs drape over the empty food tins that serve as plant pots, fading in the sun.

The woman invites me in, happily, to drink *mate* with her, offering me sickly-sweet *buñuelo* fritters that fill my mouth with sandy powder. I chew and smile, swing my feet, and stare at my white sneakers. I remember my feet as a girl, tanned from the sun. I ruminate the way cows do, treasuring memories.

The house is whitewashed adobe, neat and sturdy. They've decorated the walls in the living room with a cork-print pattern in deep red. Everything is simple and unadorned, essential. The rustle of eucalyptus leaves steals through the window. Rather than trapping the sun, the kitchen traps shade, defending itself from the heat.

My parents' house has windows on all sides and a park where trees grow, pretentiously named in Latin. It was designed by a famous gardener and then reinterpreted by my father, who every so often repeats proudly that it contains over a hundred species. A hundred species! He murmurs greedily: *Crataegus monogyna, Lagerstroemia indica, Populus alba*, and my mouth becomes full of syllables and plants. Flowering bushes are part of the architecture of the house; the trees create perspectives, draw lines, juxtapose tones and textures, hide the garage and work areas, rise up at the corners, and get bigger toward the countryside separating nature from the landscape.

In the afternoons, Jorge's mother dampens down the yard, sweeps it without raising a speck of dust: the trodden earth is like stone. With the remaining water she sprinkles the plants and tosses scraps of food to the hens, who, when they see her coming, gather in a clucking assembly.

My mother has someone who cuts the grass, which is as soft as a carpet, and she spends her afternoons watering the roses. A hummingbird drinks from the iridescent parabola of water drops that set the petals ablaze, the great kiskadees dive down into the liquid mirror of the pool. My mother doesn't cook or clean, she doesn't bother about us. She's pretty and distant. She's never happy.

Her motto is, "Why be happy when you can be unhappy?"

My mother, not mom.

Red-faced from the heat, I leave my bike on the hard earth of the yard and Jorge and I hide among the sunflowers. Huge yellow heads, rough little leaves, all parched. Pungent furrows of dark earth. A combine harvester sleeps its dinosaur *siesta*.

I don't know what we talk about, nor do I care; it's one of those meandering and unforced conversations that are so rare, a comforting dialogue.

Jorge is my only friend in the summer and being with him does me good. How old are we? I'm no more than nine, maybe he's a bit older. I have to be home promptly; if my mother finds out about these escapades, I'm doomed. I've forgotten Jorge's face, but I remember the feeling I have when we're together. It's not love, it's nothing like that, it's something maybe more precious and rare: a sweet friendship. Suddenly we fall silent, and the chorus of cicadas also stops. I feel the moment of perfection, a whole life beside him unfolds before me.

When we're grown up, I say to him, we'll still be friends.

He sits up and looks at me. No, he replies sadly. When we're grown-ups you and I will never cross paths again.

I think about his house, about mine. About the word border.

"Recordar," *remember*, from the Latin, means to bring back to the heart.

"Nostalgia" comes from the Greek, *nostos*, return, and *algos*, a medical term for "pain." Is return an illness? Does it hurt?

"Añoranza," *longing*, is loaned from Catalan.

"Agostar," *to parch in the heat of August*, a word I won't be able to understand until I change hemispheres. August, in the South, is wintertime.

When I'm older, I'll ask about Jorge again. He remembers you, they tell me. He married a schoolteacher, they also tell me. I'd like to see him, but I don't go looking for him.

I ride home nibbling at a tomato that I pulled up from the vegetable garden. I bite into its skin with my front teeth, suck out a juice that's almost sweet. It's a delicate ritual operation. I savor it with my right hand, left hand on the handlebars; I want to adjust my head to new perspectives, see from another angle.

The tomato, which left América with Hernán Cortés, wasn't red, but yellow, which is why it's called *pomo d'oro*, golden apple, in Italy. As tends to happen with the skin of immigrants, its color aroused suspicion and it was relegated to mere decoration, and didn't become the color that pulses in my mouth until the nineteenth century. These secret histories fascinate me. What's hidden in small things.

When I'm older, every time I hear a cicada those *siestas* with Jorge will come back to me; the sounds of the countryside devour time. The cicadas with their kettle drums, ardent males competing for orchestral supremacy, music-loving females patiently listening to them until, from a long way off, they discern who has the leading voice. When they find him, they mate with him. Choose a partner.

Ever since childhood, I've loved listening. I'm like a giant eardrum onto which other people's stories fall, one drop at a time; I perceive their emphasis, their happiness, their horror; I intuit what lies beneath. I'm a huntress of lives. I jot things down in a notebook, laying the lives out on paper; with a sharp-pointed pencil I rummage through their hearts.

I write at nighttime. The dark sky gradually lights up with stars and the silence around me makes every noise more intense.

When do we become separated from nature? At what point do we imagine ourselves as distinct, in opposition? She and us? I look at myself in the mirror and an astonished animal looks back at me, a fish is stranded in mercury, a lizard darts about. We're monkeys capable of bestowing names, beings open to enthusiasm. The elemental joy of existing, the body's undimmed delight, that vital reconnection to the ground beneath our feet. Galloping heightens our awareness, frees it; a bird makes it fly. As I walk, I sense we also form part of this stubborn and natural garden; to observe it is to observe ourselves.

These lines of poetry accompany me: "Tired / for lack of antennae / and not having an eye in each shoulder blade [. . .] tired / above all of always being with myself [. . .] as if I had no desire [. . .] to caress the earth with a caterpillar belly / and live for a few months / inside a stone."[3]

And an amphibian desire, a nostalgia, such longing for our animal body glimpsed in myths: a centaur, a werewolf, a mermaid, an angel.

"My name is Mary Katherine Blackwood. I am eighteen years old, and I live with my sister Constance. I have often thought that with any luck at all I could have been born a werewolf, because the two middle fingers on both my hands are the same length, but I have had to be content with what I had."[4]

Before lunch, a huge cropduster zooms past, spraying the countryside; the plane nose-dives until it brushes the earth; like an acrobat it sweeps low over the crops and rises up again. I had a friend whose dad was one of those pilots, and it seemed to me that he was the son of an angel.

The smell of pesticide. I know about the effect it has on our devastated earth, but I love how the poison smells. The perfume of Flit fly spray. The machine that goes pff-pff, like shooing away a cat. Before lunch my mother shuts all the windows and Haydée comes along, pumping out a cloud of aphrodisiac insecticide. The drops fall heavily to the ground, where moribund flies writhe and buzz, their wings feebly splayed out. I have to sit on the porch, getting bored, until all the insects have been eliminated.

They say flies live for twenty-eight days; I think they're

3 | Oliverio Girondo, "Cansancio" [Tiredness], excerpt trans. Fiona Mackintosh

4 | Shirley Jackson, *We Have Always Lived in the Castle*.

eternal. When I arrive at summer houses I see them by the window, feet in the air, dark stains on the hard mud floor. A while later I come by again and they've disappeared: flies resuscitate. I imagine them copulating shamelessly and I also picture them in the village butcher shop, stuck to a sticky strip of yellow paper, their desperate, agonizing buzz.

It's so easy to be blind to the suffering of those we don't identify with. Why are we repelled by insects?

If we were granted the power of reading the present in all its richness, we would be capable of knowing the future, as so many telltale signs appear in these childhood scenes. Pesticides and their pernicious effects, our ignorance in those days. Rachel Carson wrote: "For the first time in the history of the world, every human being is now subjected to contact with dangerous chemicals, from the moment of conception until death. They have been found in fish in remote mountain lakes, in earthworms burrowing in soil, in the eggs of birds—and in man himself. For these chemicals are now stored in the bodies of the vast majority of human beings. They occur in the mother's milk, and probably in the tissues of the unborn child."[5]

Rachel Carson was the pioneer of environmentalism and she spent hours submerged in contaminated water researching the effects of pesticides. She died of cancer. When she published her research into the effects of DDT she was attacked by the agrochemical industry. A former Secretary of Agriculture even wrote: "Since she's never married, despite being physically attractive, she's probably a communist."[6]

5 | Rachel Carson, *Silent Spring*.

6 | Editor's note: while this quote has been widely attributed to former US Secretary of Agriculture Ezra Taft Benson, his actual words in a letter to President Dwight Eisenhower were "Why a spinster with no children was so concerned about genetics?" and that she was "probably a communist." See Linda Lear, *Rachel Carson: Witness for Nature* (New York: Henry Holt, 1997), 429.

In 1951, she published *The Sea Around Us* and commented on how it was received: "People often seem to be surprised that a woman should have written a book about the sea. This is particularly true, I find, of men. Perhaps they have been accustomed for a long time to thinking about the more exciting fields of science as exclusively masculine domains. In fact, one of my correspondents a few days ago addressed me as 'Dear Sir,' explaining that although he knew perfectly well that I was a woman, he simply could not bring himself to acknowledge the fact."

I don't know whether this anecdote makes me want to laugh or cry.

Haydée and her blue sneakers; her humble yet sly look. She practiced a higher form of intelligence: that of kindness. She addressed me familiarly as *vos*, I called her *usted*. When I began using the familiar *vos* with her, she—just to underline the unbridgeable gap between us—did the opposite. She was widowed young, with two children who she raised alone. Her cooking is sublime. Homemade pasta, quince pastries, pan-fried *tortas* on rainy days. Hers is my olfactory memory; rain will always smell of Haydée's recipes. No one sits in Mamá's asymmetrical drawing room, but I'll sit with Haydée in her kitchen, we'll talk endlessly when we're both older. When Mamá dies, she'll say: "Your mother, always so punctual, everything at precisely the right time, but so on edge. What was the point?" My childhood's severity crumbles.

Lying face up on the lawn, in this long night, I feel like I could fall into the darkness full of stars. Space will soon be filled with satellites, and we won't know if what we can make out is manmade or has been floating there since the dawn of time. For now, the night is still unspoiled. When Neil

Armstrong stepped on the moon, he declared: "That's one small step for a man, one giant leap for mankind." It's partly true, but he forgot to mention the vast number of life forms that touched the surface of the moon along with him. We're not the only ones who traveled through space, other tiny forms came with the astronaut; life is ever-expanding and as soon as it takes hold in a new territory it runs wild.

We are the most wasteful species on the planet; we consume our energy reserves to keep expanding, but traveling to space can also be a way for the Earth to sow her seeds. With us, or without us, life will take its time and keep moving forward.

Is this called hope?

I saw the sea for the first time when I was nine years old, during a freezing winter vacation when my parents decided to go traveling with a couple they knew and their four children. Along with us five, that made for an unruly jumble of kids, feelings, and feuds. The adults slept in the house and they put us up in the garage. I'll never forget that damp cold rolling in off the sea or that sleepless night.

In the afternoon, I'd discovered that the Earth was ancient. Thousands of years before, on that wintry beach, someone would have seen that very same landscape, the breakers, the present buried in that unalterable mass.

On the beach I found a pilot's shoe, the stump of a mast, debris from a shipwreck, a piece of polished glass from a bottle with a message, a stone with hundreds of compacted seashells; I saw infinite time and space as primitive man might have seen them, the sand worn by erosion, I saw molluscs enamored of their rocks, I saw—or imagined I saw—marine trenches, blind fish, sea monsters, millennia beating against the waves, primordial soup.

If we were to draw a map from a fish's perspective, what would that world be like?

I raced into the sea with my shoes on. When I got home again, I put them by the fire to dry out and the leather shrank, cracked, and I was left barefoot.

On that trip I learned a lot about eternity, things you can't put into words, the need to carry spare shoes, how badly fire and leather, damp and cold go together, and furthermore, I learned to fight like a boy.

The distant proximity of certain memories, their persistence; what is irredeemably lost, what we modify, and what stays with us. I reflect on the passage of time, the passing of living beings, our built-in obsolescence, pathological anthropocentrism, I think about other beings who populate the planet. An insect lives for a day, a tree can reach 9,500 years, a tortoise 300. A bivalve Icelandic mollusc that was 507 died when scientists opened it up to study it.

If I lived on the moon I'd see the sun rise and set every ninety minutes; I could take in both poles at once and pass from one ocean to another without turning my head. I'd see twilight over America and dawn over Australia, I could perceive our "house," which, seen from the moon, would look intensely blue. A house with no religious or political borders, a global home. I guess, too, that if I could run faster than the speed of light, I could get back to my eleven-year-old self stretched out on the steaming green grass, clinging to the blades to stop myself falling toward the stars. I tell all these things to myself. And I also think that whenever I write, I reign over time.

In the tropics, fireflies dart over fields of rice, millions of specks of light appear once a year and suspend their synchronized beauty two meters above the ground. Among the shadows, I admire these tiny lanterns twinkling in the bushes. I cup them in my hand, study them, and let them go.

The countryside is a place of migrations and surprises.

The monarch butterflies have arrived, and their coppery orange has taken up residence among the eucalyptus trees. Black bodies mottled with white, tiny restless feet, fluttering wings; this memory will unite the word "lepidoptera"—so appealing, so *golosa*—to the blue butterflies baptized by Nabokov.

With their experience as hunted animals, ducks fly high; swans and flamingos are mirrored in the lake; little delicate wading birds stroll at the water's edge; behind the cattails, mud hens chatter.

So, too, do Mamá and Papá's friends arrive: with much fluttering, waving of appetizers, and pecks on the cheek.

I've managed to get away from my four siblings; my mother sunbathes, knits and reads under the trees. She doesn't swim in the pool. For some mysterious reason, she never goes swimming; she's a plant that waters itself with the hose. Nor does she wear a normal swimsuit: the dressmaker makes them for her, and they're like a kind of elegant minidress that modestly covers her whole pubic area. However, I do remember her among sparkling drops, swimming; at some point she was happier. Now she sprays herself, hides behind her dark glasses, then waters herself again. Burns to a crisp. We're not yet afraid of the sun and the rain is that miracle smelling of ozone. My lizard-mother.

My father and I go out on horseback.

"If there's clover," he says, "the land has iron. Thistles only grow in good soil. That pasture is a sign of underlying water. Never buy a plot called 'The Lagoon' where there's no sign of water, because some day it'll flood."

My father dispenses words of wisdom and I'm so small my feet don't reach the stirrups. The sun is burning. I go on horseback, I don't go horse-riding—going on horseback is like going for a walk, horse-riding is making the animal submit. Papá also says: Like this, see? We hold the reins in our left hand. Like the Arabs. That's why they conquered Spain, they were incredible horse-riders and kept their right hands free for brandishing their scimitars. And they cut the air with their whip: swish, swish. As opposed to medieval knights, with both hands holding the reins and covered head to foot in tin... Imagine that.

He also says:

"Borges knew nothing about the countryside. All his stories take place in summer, what a tourist."

Or:

"In 'The South,' Borges turns gauchos into quarrelsome thugs, but gauchos are kind and decent. He confuses them with *compadritos*, urbanized gauchos. Pure stereotypes."

He talks to himself. My response doesn't interest him or even matter to him, and this is something I'll find in so many men: he only listens to himself.

Borges won't be the only subject on which we don't see eye to eye.

In my memories it's always summertime. Cows poke their horns out from among heads of millet; they come closer cautiously and study us. I start singing and they walk toward us, they're curious, or fond of music. We inspect one another with the empathy and suspicion of beings belonging to different species. What does the cow think about when she looks at me? How does she see the world? What does she wonder? Papá likes music, but his singing is awful. In a lowing ladies' convention, the cows congregate around the watering place; there's no shade to protect them. Alfalfa, sunflowers, razor-sharp corn leaves whipping the horses' stomachs. Pampas grass and reeds in the *cañadón,* the ravine, sky in the water's depths, the silvery cry of southern lapwings.

Almost among clouds, the landscape unfolds in the limitless space of the pampa, the sun keeps tenaciously rising. I'm wearing shorts and espadrilles; when I get back home my legs are covered in thistles. I pull them out carefully with tweezers, but some are stuck, and leave marks. Like Papá's words.

I saddle and unsaddle the horse with lost words: fleece, saddle blanket, cinch, billet, fenders, and latigo strap. Better, stock saddle. Bit, headstall, curb chain. Horses' coats: chestnut, piebald, tobiano, bald face, dun. In passionate symbiosis with the animal, I gallop alone until sundown, then I abandon my centaur state, head home, and unsaddle. Beside the horse, I'm just a human. I talk to him, stroke him, thank him. He seems to nod. A bucketful of water over his back, bracing freshness. I groom him. The animal's shivering skin, recoiling; I take off his halter, watch his happy trot as he feels released, his shining powerful flanks as he moves away. Suddenly he stops, turns his head and looks at me, as if to say, "Are you still there?"

I store away words that smell of the countryside and of animals, and that when I'm far away, nobody will share with me. I won't write about these things.

If it rains, I put on one of my father's raincoats that goes down to my feet, gumboots, and open the bat wings of Aunt Juana's umbrella. I never knew her, she belongs to that troop of great family legends who the grown-ups tell stories about and who we've never met. Those mythical beings always appear foreshortened in my imagination. *La tía* Juana dressed in black, thickset, her hooked nose meeting her chin. Why did she use a man's umbrella? Why such a gothic one? None of this is explained in the grown-ups' stories. When the raindrops slacken off, I close the dearly departed's umbrella, and follow cattle tracks among the thistles. All I'm frightened of is the owls and their uncanny screech. There's a full moon: a hare is startled and streaks across the landscape, a partridge suddenly claps its wings. The clamor of the countryside.

I see myself at a distance in time and space, almost adolescent, followed by my two cats. I've cut their tail fur in the shape of a saw blade, and when they straighten their tails out, they're all spiky. I have three sweet, tame ostriches who follow me around pecking at the lawn. Also a dog. My sister hides a falcon in the wardrobe. When I want to get my clothes out, the falcon, *chimango,* opens its wings and screeches at me. It's threatening, but docile; like a trained goshawk, it will climb onto my arm. My younger sister lives in her own parallel world. I do too, and I escape at night; thinking back, I resemble a Shirley Jackson character. When I read her, I will identify with her women—we're stitched together with a mysterious thread.

My first lesson in feminism is learned from *ñandús*, those ostriches born of an unholy alliance between a bird and a horse, who can't fly but swim, run like shooting stars, and strut majestically across the pampa. Peaceful and haughty flocks with powerful feet, flexible necks, gray eyes, and the eyelashes of a diva. I study them, lose myself in them, look after the odd chick that seems lost, learn about their habits. They're curious animals who like trying to catch anything shiny. When I go out for a walk the chicks follow me; I'm part of the flock. If they sleep, they put their little heads in my lap. *Ñandús* are polygamous and when the mating season comes around, they build a nest where all the females lay such huge eggs that with a single one you could make a *tortilla española* for six people. Once their laborious task has been accomplished, they saunter off elsewhere for a chat. Now, in a curious kind of natural parity, the male *ñandú* takes charge of incubating the egg and bringing up the young.

It's said that, as well as being human, we're also the animal we carry within. There are gazelles, cats, eagles hidden inside our skeleton. Spiders and vipers. In a former life, I was an ostrich. I'll write a story about this desire; this rampant zoological nostalgia will be part of my identity, with gray eyes, long legs, and stunning feathers.

After having lunch, my older sister and I take a bucket of leftovers to where don Juan lives. He's an affectionate *criollo*, verging on old, who at some point earned his living breaking in horses. Across from his ranch, painted indigo blue, there's a tethering post for unbroken horses, which are now tamed by younger men. He's taken so many falls that he's got a bit of a limp. He likes to chat and sit down with us to look at the landscape. The landscape is the endless, shimmering plain, the limit of the horizon. I settle myself down next to don Juan and we drink *mate*. He sleeps on a camp bed, he hardly has any furniture. The iron stove is always lit, he heats his water over its embers. His room holds treasures: a woven bag full of stone balls the Indians would use to defend themselves. I picked them up in the countryside, he tells us, there are masses of them. I roll them around, my tiny hands weighed down with history. *Criollos* still use them for lassoing cattle.

In the *cañadón*, that low-lying paddock that has almost

sunk into a lagoon, the earth has never been plowed; it's preserved its botanical identity since the world began. My father refuses to touch it, he says it's where nature hoards things, her storeroom. In the distance, over clumps of stiff grass, we see a rickety wooden train go by that brings lost settlements closer; like inverted exclamation marks, windmills drawing water repeat their metallic grinding on the horizon.

Don Juan pulls more stones from the bag, shows us the groove where they'd tie a leather strap around for throwing them; Catapults, he says. Thrown weapons, *boleadoras*; one of those stones, expertly thrown, could knock your brains out, they're more effective than firearms.

These lands belonged to the Indian chief Calfulcurá. When I hear this, my head fills with images; the distant past is so remote in this zone, and yet so close. I think—later on I'll think—that don Juan's world is very similar to that of the *criollos* in Borges's story "The South," and that gauchos like him no longer exist. I suspect my father was right.

I concentrate on the words I must learn to describe this vanishing world; I treasure them, I write a parallel dictionary, they're a secret code, without them I couldn't go back. Don Juan also declares that his *puchero* is the best stew around, and that women ruin knives. Like all *criollos*, he carries a knife at his back, strapped around his waist. He wears a beret or a tilted sombrero, espadrilles. If it's Sunday, he puts on his boots, and, over his waistband, a belt with silver coins. In the countryside, knives are used for everything. He grumbles as he whets the blade against a stone; the blade whistles, he teaches me always to cut on the bias. Sharp knives and skeletal greyhounds are don Juan's attributes. In winter and summer, he gets up at sunrise and cooks beef over the fire for the men who work the land—they eat without a plate, just using their knives, their teeth, and a hunk of bread. Once they leave, he cleans and sorts out the horses' tack, and at noon has lunch ready for the men. A world without women. There's no running water, the men wash their feet in a drum of freezing cold water. Stroking the greyhounds' heads, my sister and I share out the leftovers. The dogs delightedly slap our bare legs with their tails. Don Juan has benches made from cows' hip bones covered in sheepskins, he uses polished horns as spoons; in that elemental world everything is recycled. With thin strips of leather, he crafts headstalls and reins for the horses, sometimes he adds silver side trappings and the yard fills with sparkling light. He rummages in a chest and pulls out a flower made from straw, his school notebooks, a map. What beautiful handwriting. He teaches us sayings: "Wind from the East, rain on man and beast." "South dark, North clear, rain is near."

Behind the house, toward the Italian neighborhood, the eucalyptus trees release their watery rustle.

Sleepy, the dogs leave off barking.

Death in the countryside. Flies busy themselves on the mastodontic cadaver of a cow. Even before setting eyes on the putrefying corpse, my horse balks at the sickly-sweet smell of decomposition. Death is vaster in the pampa. I dig my heels into the horse, who whinnies and shies away.

There's life in death. White grubs writhe, having waited inside the cow's stomach for the moment to begin their work; jet-black blowflies choose a spot to lay their eggs. The cow's eyes have dulled and are coming out of their sockets, they look like ping pong balls covered with a silk stocking. The cow's tongue is swollen, its body like a balloon, legs stiff like cardboard.

Overhead, the huge gravedigging birds of prey are circling. Vultures. A *chimango* wrestles with a piece of something I prefer not to see, it jumps triumphantly up and down on the grass, while others chase it hoping to seize its prey. Spirals in the sky, the limpid flight of the peregrine falcon. When the bird sees its prey, it can plummet from the sky like a stone. Patiently, the dead cow awaits its fate, no other funeral rites are foreseen. In a few weeks it will still be there, but with its skin all stuck to the bone, the frenzy of death gone. After the bubbling corpse will come the sunken calm of the skeleton. A sight both magnificent and repugnant.

Death is the main provider of nutrients for the soil, we feed it before we leave, we return to the underworld like Odysseus, we go down to hell thanks to decomposers that rain down overflowing energy that soaks into the earth entrusted with breaking things down, transporting and nurturing. We only see what goes on above ground, but a large part of life's activities take place beneath the surface. If we put our ear to the ground we hear the world's pulse: fungi metabolize waste and corpses, they get to work on the dead animal and also on moldy bread, on the forgotten orange with its dusty green efflorescence, they travel the world in the form of spores carried on the air. From them everything grows, implacably, generation after generation. They are the great recyclers. Carbon dioxide, ammonia, phosphorus, nitrogen, and countless other ingredients become available to the surrounding area. Eager for such tasty "snacks" as living tissue and skin on sweaty feet, ringworm and other minuscule parasitic beings chomp away industriously on vines, toenails, hair, bread, fruit, rind. Without fungi and bacteria we would be pure waste. Human beings have discovered that recycling can be one of our paths to salvation; fungi have known this for four hundred million years.

"How ridiculous to go saving whales," my father says, unmoved by dead animals. "What's the point of them? What we should be saving is worms. All the humus in the countryside is produced by worms."

"Humor," "humus," "humility," "human."
Related words. A potter made us from clay.
Everything is a return.

Life in death. Intermediate states. The energy of destruction, the return to the origin. When is a body definitively dead? Does calmness come? Life, too, is one long question about our disappearance. Crazed by pain, we dance and wail at the onset of loss. Meanwhile, flesh displays its own ending, germinates and breaks down until it becomes compost. Neither living, nor dead, intermediate beings produce horror and literature. Vampires, zombies. But, when everything calms down, what is dirty becomes clean, what was broken down is reborn, time sculpts skulls that no longer inspire fear. Nobody trembles at a skeleton, it ceases to be food for pain or fodder for magic and becomes an incitement to philosophy. And good old Hamlet, with his plain and simple skull.

To be, or not to be.

To be part of a whole.

The summer is spent taking food for don Juan's greyhounds, stroking their heads, calling them by name, pandering to their whims. But one day we come bearing gifts and our arrival is not greeted by joyous barking: we approach their silence and they are lying on the dusty ground, apparently asleep, each with a bullet in their head. The chains that tether them are absurd, painful, bloodstained, no one has bothered to free them, this imprisonment in death is an atrocious image. A shotgun leans against a tree.

Don Juan clarifies perfectly naturally: "They killed a hen." We look at him, sobbing, and scream: "You murderer!" The old man doesn't understand. "Those dogs had got a taste for flesh," he repeats. "They'd kill again, a hen. . ." He doesn't know how to explain.

You can eat a hen. But not a dog. For him, greyhounds are working dogs, hunters. The pelts of hares sell very well, but a hen is worth more.

Worlds apart.

Something is broken.

Rebirth.

Young embryos of birds, caimans, pigs, and humans are similar to one another. Also, what gestates in a mother's womb has the semblance of a fern, we develop from an egg, at a certain point we have gills. Living matter replicates itself, we are related to fish. Perhaps flowers attract our attention because they recall our insect era, we drool and buzz at the sight of pollen.

I like thinking of myself that way, part of a chain.

I read that in the United States, there are people who hand the body of a loved one over to be composted. I'm struck by this.

You're dust, and to dust you'll return.

Is childhood also recycled? Where does it go? Are we part of the same tree, copies of an original trunk? How are the branches that sheltered us preserved in us, the stories that gave us shade?

My father had a curious way of seeing life: serious and ironic at the same time, cultured and popular. I didn't like asking him too many things because, enamored by his own ideas, he was always going back to the origins, and the simplest explanation could become a whole tiresome volume of an encyclopedia. However, I struggled to disassemble some of his stories, which for years I took to be true. He told me, for example, that Álvar Núñez Cabeza de Vaca had been the first Latin American tourist. One day he'd gone out for a walk and, just strolling along, had come across the Iguazú Falls, which, in Guaraní, means "big water." That abundant river dashes itself against the rocks, blurring the landscape to mist with its never-ending spray. Suspended droplets, eternal rainbow, roaring water. Listening to my father, I naïvely imagined the military man with his armor, sword, and a backpack. With weapons, but also a picnic hamper. I imagined the Tupi-Guaranís, in a peaceful procession, accompanying the conquistador. I imagined him, relaxed or amazed, discovering the wondrous sight. Maybe even taking a photo of it? I imagined this arch-conquistador benignly paving the way for tourists. Now, as I write this, I laugh all over again.

Et in Arcadia ego.

To dream of a happy place. The garden, its walls that keep danger at bay, ecological utopia. The past is always better, we require some distance to find ourselves. But don't we always carry ourselves with us? We destroy nature to live and at the same time fantasize about returning to mother earth, who will shelter us and make us happy. Ideas and concepts that we've been repeating since the dawn of time, commonplaces that articulate our thoughts. "Protection!" we poor humans groan, weary of struggling, "a moment's rest!" Does this dreamt-of place exist? Where does this garden grow?

For the Romans, persecuted and persecuting at the outer reaches of their empire, the dream of domesticated nature was a fountain from which flowed the most calming fantasies. Leisure, *ocio*, and its negation, business, *negocio*.

"Happy the man who lives remote from business, after the manner of the ancient race of mortals";[7] dreams of a perfect life within nature that accompany us from Eden onwards. And "how tranquil is the life," of course, if we don't have to milk cows, or look at the sky to see if rain will bring us bread. If we don't have a demanding master or boss. Or suffer cold, heat, or hunger. Or a back bent double from pounding the earth. A dream of a poetic ideal. Shade from trees, water from a spring, a flower-studded meadow; happiness and calm.

"On contours of the hill," says Friar Luis, "I have an orchard planted by my hand, / and in the spring when still / its lovely flowers stand, / they offer proof that fruit will fill the land."[8] What a sunny meditation. But every paradise has its serpent; even the *locus amoenus*, in which [Giovanni] Bocaccio was also escaping from the plague. We fantasize about an escape that never happens, we are children of Horace the dreamer, of the *carpe diem*. The Marquis of Santillana and his "blessed be those who with the hoe sustain their lives and live content."[9] Garcilaso [de la Vega]'s gentle lovelorn shepherds and, lastly, *beatus ille*, Marcela the shepherdess. Behind her, poking fun, the intelligent and infectious laughter of [Miguel de] Cervantes.

Whoever writes recycles memories, pilfers scraps, revives and corrects them. Stories about to germinate that

7 | Horace, "Epodes," trans. William Shepherd.

8 | Friar Luis de León, "Secluded Life," trans. Willis Barnstone.

9 | Marquis of Santillana, "Loa de los oficios serviles" [In Praise of Humble Work], excerpt trans. Fiona Mackintosh.

yield up their content and nutrients, their peculiar nitrogen, converting the past into organic matter. Science also acts as a driving force behind these fantasies.

I'm fascinated by how science takes itself so seriously. Where would it be without imagination? Spontaneous generation, defended by Aristotle, Descartes, and Newton, their fabulous histories offer rich pickings for stories: God created Eve from Adam's rib, flesh transforms into maggots, insects emerge from decomposed vegetable matter, rats are born from dirty underwear, fireflies from sparkling morning dew. Birds emerge from fruits, ducks come out of seashells, and fir trees, when exposed to sea salt, produce geese. Beautiful explanations that once were called science and now seem to us like surrealist images, metaphors, poems, stories. The earth was flat for centuries on end; the most unknown continent is the one that lies between our ears. We suspect animals can't ponder their own existence, but we don't know for sure, they share a large part of their genome with us. Who can tell us our ways of thinking don't feed off childish dreams? We can't think about ourselves outside our own thoughts, which makes all our ideas tautological. Nevertheless, every age arrogantly assumes that its scientific truths are absolute.

I wander and divigate; my feet sharpen my mind. In the horizontal vertigo of the pampa, the straight line takes on a foundational power. What causes this emotion?

"There is an hour in the evening when the plain seems to say something or says it infinitely, and we never understand it."[10]

I walk with my feet tapping against the world's crust,

10 | Jorge Luis Borges, "El Fin" [The End], excerpt trans. Fiona Mackintosh.

I imagine what's going on underneath, I endow minute things with presence. A woven mystery, a network, an infinite resonance.

We're the product of interwoven alliances. Maurice Blanchot writes: "Yes, happily language is a thing, a written thing, a piece of bark, a splinter of stone, a fragment of clay in which the reality of the earth subsists."

Like other life forms, literature survives, connects, colonizes. Cellulose fibers are converted into paper, into books, and immortal words. Words, too, provide compost. So are intertexts our way of recycling literature? Of metabolizing it?

One book belongs to another.

Growing. Hiding from adults, getting away from my house and its squabbles, climbing up into the acacias to read, stockading myself with books, activating the mechanisms of disarmament. Thinking and recomposing, inhabiting mysterious territories, being uncomfortable. Pain is fertile, with its dark consistency. I value lack as a form of apprenticeship, and discomfort. Plants that cling to the rock to withstand the wind, a species that evolves to survive and develops incredible strategies, feet that walk out from the sea and drag themselves on land, wings that sprout to flee.

Maybe Darwin not only discovered the laws of natural selection, but also opened the door to another kind of reflection: we only evolve through what we lack.

I take stock of what I lack and develop a stubborn optimism.

There was also the immense city, beautifully tree-lined, a flat windswept territory in which someone, considered to be "head gardener of the city," invented shade. I'm sitting in a plaza in Buenos Aires beneath the muscly limbs of a magnolia, I flit from one idea to another, letting my mind wander. The magnolia tree beneath which I took my first steps, and then learned to ride a bicycle. Beneath which I met my friends in those long-gone soppy days of romantic love.

The man who planted it would plant over 150,000 trees in the city. His name was Charles Thays, he became Carlos when he emigrated; he was born in Paris in 1849 and died in Buenos Aires. One single man changed the landscape, protected us from the sun, without him this city would not be that city I long for.

Thays gave us the gift of oxygen. He abandoned the habit of planting in a European style and also used native flora whose names the conquistadors wouldn't know how to spell. He designed parks and plazas, gardens for the rich and leisure spaces for those who weren't. He said: "It's better to live in a forest hut than in a palace without a garden."

There's one thing about Buenos Aires I really long for, now that I live far away: its violet streets at the end of November, the *jacarandás*. The *yacara'na*, a name that comes from the Tupi language of Brazil. What's the plural? They do exist in Spain, but there are fewer, their difference is marked by the change of grammatical gender and accentuation: *las jacarandas*. But *los jacarandás* (or jacarandae) to me conjures up a multitude of trees with an accent on their last syllable.

The memory of plants, their fragrance, their sound. I cross the plaza that is delicately roofed in violet blue; in a few weeks the flowers will fall to the pavement and go from canopy to carpet. The *jacarandá*, miraculous after rain, its gentle trembling, dark gray trunk and branches, as sturdy as nostalgia. They are the last gasp of freedom before going into school.

The nicest thing is the huge playground, with a wisteria threaded through it; the school building is more severe than elegant and has bars on the windows. Since I write well, they pick me to keep a diary; it's the first time I've ever been entrusted with such a task. I'm not one of the best students, I'm not interested in anything apart from literature and I cultivate a supreme indifference that protects me from stiffness and boredom.

This first-ever commission makes me feel special and I set to writing with a passion. I write in a large notebook with gold-edged pages on subjects that really matter: passing seasons, falling leaves, wondrous flowering of the wisteria racemes. But when they read what I've written, they relieve me of the task.

Half a century later I'm still writing abstractedly, unmoved by fads and fashions, and those dark memories are a gothic arsenal. I write about nuns who rise from the dead in that gigantic building, built at the beginning of the twentieth century, with its vertiginous flights of stairs and handrails, its intense cold. When one of the Sisters died, they used to hold her wake in the chapel. I never peered into the coffin because I was scared; later, along the freezing corridors, the dead woman would reappear, or perhaps it wasn't the same one. I spent my childhood among devils and revenants.

The older girls play in the main playground, the little ones round the back, under an avocado tree whose crown seems to touch the sky. Every now and then, like oily green grenades, the ripe fruits launch themselves into the void and explode on the paving slabs, lying there split open, displaying their dark stone. Those unctuous green fruits are Proustian madeleines.

I think about migration and seeds, about how an immobile tree can cross continents. The ballerina lightness of thistledown, the migrating bird that has pecked the ground and whose droppings contain seeds, the pods that burst open on the ground, morning glory seeds that take the train and fill the railway tracks with blue trumpets.

The avocado stone is like a Fabergé egg. How does it travel? What animal could possibly swallow and transport it? Which one would allow such a mass to pass through its digestive tract, to sow it far from the place it was eaten? No living herbivore is capable of such a feat, but thirteen thousand years ago there were plenty. Take the glyptodon, for example, or the megatherium, a sloth the size of an elephant. In actual fact, it was the jaguar, with its distended jaws, who saved the avocado's life until another seed distributor came along: human beings. So the avocado traveled and has various names: *aguacate*, from the Nahuatl word for testicle, being similarly shaped, and also *avocato*, because in Italy, owing to its high price, only *avvocatos*, lawyers, could afford to eat it. We call it *palta*, which is a Quechua word. Whatever its name, the fruit ended up being associated with humans, but forming an alliance with humans is making a pact with the devil, since the food industry is working toward getting rid of the avocado's stone, and they will decide when, where, and how it reproduces. Poor avocado, I say to myself, while I wait for one to crash on my head: in our jaws it's at risk of extinction.

My first love also had a rural backdrop, red sunsets, and perpetual summer.

I stroll with him along the *cañadón*; he wants to be an ornithologist and he initiates me in the ways of birds. White-faced ibis, waterfowl, flamingos, and a skunk that he tries to catch and that perfumes him with pee. He belongs to a big Durrell-like family, his sister is my friend and we will remain friends to this day. Animals all over the place, Siamese fighting fish with their splendid tails, a climbing porcupine that shed its spines and with whom we shared a bed.

It's a sunny, restorative love, peacefully hopeful. Complete and all-consuming. We spend summer in the countryside and he devotes his time to putting rings on ducks. The rings are for studying migration and each one says: "Please return to the Natural History Museum." Whoever finds them can trace the animal's journey. Hidden among the reeds we capture them, ring them, and let them go again. He studies their migrations and I, at this stage, still don't know that migration will be my destiny. He is sweet and gentle, much more interesting than the other people around me. He draws, takes photographs, I admire everything he does. One day he introduces me to an English friend, also an ornithologist. "What are you going to be when you're older?" he asks me. While I fantasize, he is already saying: "I'm going to be a writer." I'm astonished by his self-assurance.

We will be together for nearly ten years. One day, chuckling slightly, he will say to me: When we get married, I'm going to give you a ring that instead of saying "Please return to the Natural History Museum" says "Please return her to me." I look at him, horrified.

We don't get married, I'll have other partners, but I'll always remember him. I'll never wear a wedding ring.

Times of study and steeliness. Of pleasure and pain. Of being young in the South while the barbarians and their dictatorships were rising. Knowing and getting to know each other. Crossing America in a rundown old car, weaving friendships that would last forever.

Almost virgin America, painful and magnificent, nature in all its splendor. So young before the horror came, so idealistic. We traveled searching for something, some "reality" that was always a bit further on. We weren't tourists, we were pilgrims, travelers.

I crossed from Buenos Aires as far as Lima, going up through a besieged Chile, the Andes, the desert, the sea. On the border, apart from the snow and gigantic mountains, we met a man who was fleeing Pinochet on foot. It was prophetic. An old young man, as we would soon become. Siege, danger, repression. I always remember that scene when I reread *Distant Star* by Roberto Bolaño. That was the climate. And such lust for life.

I slept in the railway station in Machu Picchu, overcome by beauty; I saw the flowing Urubamba, I washed dishes in the Pacific, I crossed the desert by starlight to avoid the sun's piercing rays. I spent nearly a week in Antofagasta, by the sea, protected by rosy cliffs, watching condors fly above my head; I came back passionately in love with someone who would shortly be disappeared. Repression savaged our country too.

Where must his beautiful body be, his tortured body? At the bottom of the river? Did they throw him in naked, so no one would be able to identify him? Who accompanied him on his journey? Sparkling twilight reflected in the water?

Maybe there, on the riverbed, his body stirs up clouds of golden clay and is lulled to sleep on the silt.

We traveled and loved in ramshackle buses, from Buenos Aires to Santiago, Santiago to Lima, Lima to Bolivia, we crossed rivers that swept us along, unpaved roads. We skirted precipices with a drunken driver, inconceivable roads. I often imagine his young body shrouded in seaweed, I dream of him.

But I don't want to talk about this.

Floodwaters erased the roads and the countryside was lost to greed, shirking of public responsibility, mindless cultivation of soy. The wooden train that used to go all the way down south was lost, as were the herds of horses with their thundering hooves, the flocks of ostriches. The clamor of the sky in spring was lost, along with the years and their folk. Childhood was lost, as it always is. Love was lost.

My generation was lost.

A few words suffice: I lived in a dictatorship and had to go into exile.

And the South became North.

Thanks to exile we come to know the earth.

Maria Zambrano, *La tumba de Antígona* [Antigone's Tomb]
excerpt translated by Fiona Mackintosh

north

Not the moon, or the seasons, or the smells. Not the color of the trees, or their shade. Not the language, the feelings, the sky, the birds. Not the house, the food, the fittings, furnishings, belongings. Not the humor, or the caresses, or the books. Not the twilight, or the horizon, or the horses' hair. Not the shopping list, or the songs, or the secret codes. Not the friends, or the neighbors, or love. Not the sayings, or the songs, or the children's games in the plazas. Not the plazas, or the colors, or the statues.

Everything was lost, when I turned the world on its head.

But life goes on, it imposes itself, heaping up skeletons, animal and vegetal remains, memories.

It tugs at me.

Where could I begin? In the beginning was a tree? It wouldn't be a *jacarandá*. Or an *aguaribay*. Or an *ombú*. Maybe a holm oak.

In the beginning was a holm oak.

I live on Calle Fuencarral, Madrid, in a women's boarding house where there's only one man. His breakfast is made; his bed is made. Not ours. At the market everyone else cuts in line, coming in from all sides. I wait because I don't know how to take my turn. Artichokes, peaches, and green beans have become *alcachofas*, *albaricoques*, and *judías*, instead of *alcauciles*, *damascos*, and *chauchas*. The boarding house is all in black and white, dingy and sad. An infinite corridor with a telephone at the far end where there's always someone whispering. The shared kitchen is grubby. Only one bathroom. Every time I have a shower the downstairs neighbor comes up to complain that it's raining through his ceiling.

I move to a tiny house where other people in exile start arriving, six of us in thirty square meters, it makes no difference. An attic room on Calle San Marcos with no windows facing the street. In Chueca the prostitutes cross paths with blind people and their sticks. At night, it rains, but it's not rain; I later discover that they wash the streets here.

I study a metro map with names that mean nothing to me. There's a green area, slightly further out and I say to myself: I'm going to live here. In the labyrinth of stations, that grassy blot is Casa de Campo, and I dream of reading beneath those trees. The house has dismal furniture. Although we're in a democracy now, the lady of the house has a box where she keeps vinyl records of fascist marches and photos of the Third Reich. There's a crucifix on the door. I come downstairs with my book and the lone men who wander among the trees crowd around me, so I look like bait. From the balcony I can see miraculous snow on the mountains.

I spend Christmas alone and devour a huge amount of chocolate. I drink a whole bottle of wine even though I'm practically a teetotaler. A somewhat unconvincing suicide attempt, nothing sublime, I tell myself, while my perky side mocks me. Luckily, I'm able to split myself in two: the one who suffers, the one who downplays suffering. My love life has dissolved into a series of encounters that mean nothing to me. I pull myself together. I fall apart. I'm sad. I dull the pain. I want to live.

What a gray city. No plazas with *jacarandás*, nor abandoned lots. No in-between zones, nor outsized avenues. Madrid, with its narrow little streets and old buildings, feels like a village. No nature straining to grow, the rain is barely a memory of other rains. Everything is fenced in and compact, space is at a premium. I use Retiro Park like a private garden; sometimes I go out to get away from the city. There are mountains and open countryside nearby, and the suburbs give way to and intermingle with fields of crops, unraveling into areas where sheep graze.

It takes a long time to understand new spaces, years to stop comparing them.

Now, in this world that has swung around, cold weather comes from the North and there are no glaciers in the South. "Stone-gray sky, it won't be dry," "Bring your jacket every day, at least until the end of May." "April showers brings May flowers." Celebrating my birthday in spring, not autumn. "Year of snow, crops will grow." From the balcony I see the moon wax and wane the other way around. The proverbs mean nothing to me. Where is my Southern Cross?

Cape jasmine is gardenia, cape leadwort is plumbago. The Mexican bay leaf is an oleander. The *palo borracho*, *achiras* and *lapacho* have disappeared. I confuse oak, *roble*, with holm oak, *encina*, olive trees don't speak to me. Stunted little trees, with ancient, gnarled trunks and an understated green; tiny leaves that curl up. It takes so long to relish differences.

At first I'd imagined staying out of the country for six months, then returning once the violence subsided. I receive a message: "They came looking for you, the house is destroyed." My life was saved by a matter of hours, but the border has closed.

Life is on hold, suspended.

To die in one life, and be born in another.

Since I have no room for anything else, I buy a bulb and give it a home on my table. I look at its pregnant belly, its role as storeroom, reserve, multiplier. I study its relationship to the earth, to its roots. And mine.

I'm uprooted.
And the years will go by.

Baudelaire sets off walking around Paris and inaugurates *spleen,* that feeling of someone who strolls, not among trees, but among strangers. To lose yourself, turn your gaze where no one looks, dissolving and remaking. To be far from home, and at the same time feel close. Like a wood, the big city unfolds.

"Multitude, solitude."

I walk around Madrid, there are no bars where I can read, people talk at the tops of their voices, in the neighborhood drinking dens they toss the leftovers of the tapas onto the floor. Everything is different for me, slightly aggressive. It smells of cooking oil. On the shared patio you can hear forks beating eggs in a ceramic bowl.

Walter Benjamin, the great flâneur, "goes botanizing" on the asphalt, contemplates the panorama of beautiful architecture and bustle. A "distracted gaze" that organizes the environment in another way, reinvents it.[11]

We think that "going out for a stroll" is almost innate to being human, but that's not the case, it's one thing to walk from A to B, with a particular purpose; it's something quite different to stroll.

Going for a stroll is a relatively recent activity; before the eighteenth century it wouldn't have occurred to anyone to stroll along the street, the state of the pavements, safety, or hygiene wouldn't allow it.

People did stroll, of course, but within the confines of the garden or around cloisters, a possibility open exclusively to a particular social class.

11 | Walter Benjamin, "Paris of the Second Empire in Baudelaire," trans. Howard Eiland, Edmund Jephcott, Rodney Livingston, and Harry Zohn.

Nor is strolling the same for men as for women; there are dangerous spaces where women can't go. The shame of an unchaperoned woman, who runs the risk of being mistaken for someone who "walks the streets." Likewise, strolling isn't the same for white people as for Black, for poor people as for rich; the old idea that speaking objectively is to speak from nowhere is nonsense, universals are false. To change country, I think, is to banish generalizations, to introduce nuance.

Gradually, I start falling in love with the old Madrid, its narrow streets, its past. Between the flaking paint of its walls and traces of the war I discover tiny shaded gardens. The garden of Lope de Vega's house, where I reread *Fuente Ovejuna*. This is the description given by its former owner:

"My garden, briefer than a comet's blaze, / Hath but two trees, and flowers – ten in all, / Just here two fellow nightingales do call, / Two pitchers form a fountain; o'er two stones – / Or colored shells – they let their water fall."[12]

To transplant oneself. To put down roots, somehow. Give form to what grows, situate it. Neither neatly pruned hedges, nor confused labyrinths. I could propose a game: If I were a garden, what kind of garden would I be? Wild or formal? Romantic? Would I put everything on display, or would there be hidden nooks?

There's a style of neglected garden that springs up on uncultivated land, waste ground, or spaces that are tricky to get to, and that provides a refuge. This kind of garden pops up of its own accord without anyone planting it, it has no limits or defined categories and it changes the area in unexpected and surprising ways. It is the product of many overlapping ecosystems and with its fluid energy it resists

12 | Félix Lope de Vega y Carpio, "La Filomena," excerpt trans. Fiona Mackintosh.

control, reconquering the space. A mobile garden where all norms are questioned. It's inwardly restless; soil and time shape its design. This resistant garden is called the "Third Landscape."[13] A clipping, a fragment, a refuge. Its uncertain limits are the most fertile zones. It unites territories, intersects, it is hybrid, a new space of communication.

That's how I feel.

Is there also a third landscape for the foreigner?

It's not the right time, or place, or house, or partner. I'm lacking the wherewithal to look after her, there's no one to help me. I've got nothing but a crazy happiness at the birth of my daughter. That's how, in precarity and in a foreign land, the children of exile were born. Why does literature favor death over life? Why are battles considered heroic, and not births?

I wait and trust, I respond to death with life.

I sing to creation.

I swell, germinate, blossom. Everything becomes vegetal. I dream of jungles that multiply across my notebook. I write without plan or purpose. Life strains, mightily.

Writhing, shouting, controlling the world with my breath. I reject all medication, I will not mitigate the pain. Pain? I wouldn't define it as such. Panting like a beast, dissolving myself, and being nothing but a body.

Fear and pleasure together. More than pain, effort. Giving birth was magnificent and brutal.

When the creature shows her beautiful little face I say to the midwife: I want another one.

Now.

I'm a life-giving goddess, an exhausted woman.

The baby girl crawls on my front and studies me, snuffling

13 | Gilles Clément, *Manifeste du Tiers paysage* [Manifesto of the Third Landscape].

about in the air, demanding nourishment. We look at each other for the first time.

No one comes to visit us in the hospital. We are alone.

Womb, woman, wood. Mother, material, matter. In Latin *matrix* means "pregnant female" and, in a broader sense, a trunk that puts forth shoots. Matrix and matriculation. Matriculation is an origin as well as an offshoot, a registration. To "touch wood" brings good luck.

Seed fruits of etymologies, the stories they tell us.

"Nature" comes from the Egyptian word *NTR*, which means God. I don't know how to pray, but I worship a domestic goddess on this winter's night. I imagine my own Genesis. And what if the generating principle had been a woman? It seems more logical. I imagine her making jam with the fruits of the tree of good and evil. Negotiating with Cain and Abel. We light the stove. Home and hearth.

In a circle, around the hearth, the ethic of dialogue sprang up; in this warm and protected place we learned how to tell stories. We are stories.

Words blaze and crackle in the fire.

To be torn apart and put back together, to choose and go without, to recover what was lost. Capture "what is conspicuous by its absence." Negotiate with silence, share a look and find a clearing in the memory.

I write and fill notebooks that I keep on losing.

Kafka wrote: "A book must be an ice-axe to break the frozen sea within us."[14] He belonged to a minority, he wrote in German, a language only spoken by ten percent of Czechs,

14 | Franz Kafka, "Letter to Oskar Pollak, 1904," trans. Clara Winston and Richard Winston.

he was Jewish, and he was ill. He had serious problems with women and his sisters perished in the Holocaust. Pulsing through all his work is the feeling of desolate exclusion, uprootedness, but also the desire to fly.

Like a diamond, hope.

I read "Wish to Become an Indian," a celebration of the mere fact of living, making do without any ties, in dialogue with the landscape. If I ever write something about nature, I will put this text as an epigraph.

I remember Kafka's life. What have I got to complain about?

Making friends in Madrid wasn't easy. Although *madrileños* think they're hospitable, that wasn't my experience. It depends which doors are opened, it's partly luck: the first few years were hard. Feeling they didn't need us, that we were dispensable. An experience like that changes you, teaches you to think.

I've been here three years when I make my first friend who gives me two gifts: the first is an appreciation of holm oaks, the second, he suggests I teach a class. My daughter is barely nine months old when we give our writing workshop in the countryside: I take her with me, she is almost born to this line of work that as the years go by will also become hers. We could have been carpenters, shoemakers, ironed clothes for a living, but we are artisans of words.

We are rootless, but this trade, literature, was also practiced by many members of my family. It makes it easy to travel light.

Workshops and their constant dialogue.

To teach like someone who is strolling, someone who is sowing. To earn friends along the way.

Forty years on, Toni and I are still finding one another, I think he doesn't fully understand his importance in my life. I call him and ask him to comment on these pages.

And what if each life was a landscape? If we were plains, jungles, sand dunes? There's a term that defines what I'm beginning to understand, that will, at some point, represent my lot in life: escarpments, steep slopes, terraces farmed to exhaustion, walls of stone that display beautiful sculptures of hard work. This type of cultivation is called "heroic agriculture." I find this definition that, in some way, represents me. What can you plant when your land has disappeared?

I get to know new territories, new ways of working. It isn't a young continent like the one where I was born, but rather a territory devastated by thousands of generations and plows. Terraced crops, gnarled vines, pastures.

I begin to comprehend the landscape.

Dehesa, pasture, comes from "defense"; these pastures came into being during the reconquest of Spain as a way of protecting livestock or perhaps to see more clearly who was approaching. They are woods with clearings rich in biodiversity, formed of holm oaks or cork oaks, grass, ash trees, rockrose, broom, and acorns that fall from the holm oaks to be devoured by pigs that roam wild. I tell myself that pastures are one of the best examples of a balanced collaboration between nature and humans, their intelligent and manifold usefulness, the cork oaks' twisted memory, their patient servitude.

Roots.

Deleuze and Guattari wanted to write a rhizomatic book, in which all the parts were interconnected, and you couldn't tell precisely where one piece of writing ended and another began, a fluid non-hierarchical structure, a mesh of networked meanings. I imagine the roots of cypress trees, with a definite center, pivoting, immovable, corkscrewing downwards; ivy roots (or radicants)[15] that subsist clinging to all sorts of surfaces. The pregnant bulb I kept in my first house in Madrid. What root represent me? I opt for epiphytes or aerial roots that don't require a point of origin in the earth and support themselves solely on something that can be lost: a tree, a homeland.

"Exile as identity. Foreignness as homeland. To be rooted without clinging to the earth, like an air plant."[16]

To lose your footing, change sky.

To move once is to move forever, take on the speed of things, that which falls apart in our hands, to punch a hole through reality, try and respond to questions about what has been lost. There's a relationship between this way of looking and observing a wood, which is apparently static and repetitive. Being a foreigner is like living in a space where you must interpret all the signs, where you have to be always on the alert.

The Algerian writer Malika Mokeddem and *The Men Who Walk*, her story. Mokeddem studied medicine in France and, faced with the rise of fundamentalism in her country, chose a third way, neither Algerian nor French, adopting the nomadic past of her ancestors. She thus develops an unfixed identity, one that's fluid, mixed, trans, not rigid, protean, malleable; that displays the tension between longing to put down roots and desiring to fly, between the feeling of belonging and the principle of individuation, between being true to herself

15 | Nicolas Bourriaud, *The Radicant*, trans. James Gussen and Lili Porten.

16 | Clara Obligado, *Una casa lejos de casa. La escritura extranjera* [A Home Far from Home: Foreign Writing].

and fitting established molds. As I read her, I repeat that the defenders of fixed roots forget that we human beings are not anchors.

To cast off. Overcome fear. Become rooted in the planet. Allow yourself to be borne by the wind. Germinate.

I grew up in Buenos Aires among Spaniards who didn't alter their habits, I live in Spain among Argentinians who refuse to change. An astonished Spaniard hears themself referred to as "Latino," a Latin American grudgingly tolerates the supercilious put-down "sudaca." Crossing a border means changing forever, and that truth only becomes obvious years later; the emigrant is the most Proustian of beings, always in search of "a lost time." There are other borders too: of gender, class, local urban geography, dangerous streets that we, as women, can't cross. The simple displacement from one's small town to the big city; "emigrations," sometimes so costly, within one's own country; moving house. In some way, we are all being uprooted. I jot down in my notebook: to write is to take root in the air.

"Exotic," according to the dictionary of the Spanish Royal Academy: "Foreign or originating from a distant country or place, perceived as very different within one's own. 2. adj. Strange, shocking, extravagant."

I make up my own definition. "Exotic: what is not me. That into which I have converted myself. The Spaniards, for me."

Also, according to the Spanish Royal Academy, I'm an "exotic species," that is to say: "Species or subspecies that survives or reproduces beyond its natural range of distribution."

The market is full of "exotic" goods: ravioli, which a grocer proposes to fry because he thinks they are little meat pies, like our *empanadas*. Papayas, avocados, pineapples, *chirimoyas*. Food brings bring new flavors and perspectives, they change us from within.

I try to get a passport for my daughter, but they won't give me one. She was born here, but her parents are not Spanish. She's not so much exotic as stateless.

In the pine forest, the interminable trunks weave gothic arches and among their dark columns we gather pine cones to light the fireplace. The wind picks up and the pine trees start dancing, whispering a watery music that the locals call "marejadilla," a slight swell. People say trees don't move, but these pines dance and curve downward toward the earth, their needles tremble, the pine cones fall scattering their seeds to the wind, they reproduce far away. Pine roots keep them in the place they were born. Yet they have colonized the earth, they settle in the most inhospitable places with extraordinary vigor. The Scotch pine, with its ramrod-straight endless trunk, its itinerant destiny as a ship's mast.

There's no civilization without trees. When I light the fireplace, the pine cones' tongues are gifts of fire.

It's getting dark, and I see a cloud of smoke. In the center, a blazing fist. The whole day long, after the black smoke, the sky turns a copper color. Forest fire: a journey straight from paradise to inferno.

My nephew, who's a physicist, writes me a letter telling me about trees and their virtues:

> Their first problem was going from single-cell organisms to larger structures because, as they grew,

they became unstable. So they developed specialized organs: roots or trunks; they had to optimize their absorption of the sun's energy and carbon dioxide from the atmosphere, which is difficult to do without the tree ending up unfeasibly heavy. Absorption of sunlight depends on the amount of surface area exposed to the sun, and on the tree's weight and volume. It's an incredible idea: the leaves are distributed in a fractal pattern, which augments the surface area without altering the volume. But this solution creates a further problem for them: withstanding the wind, since the greater the surface area exposed, the greater the drag. And so they come up with another perfect solution: their branches bend. But the interaction with the atmosphere goes beyond a problem of energy. Trees display incredibly complex aerodynamic shapes depending on the functions they need to carry out. For example, deciduous trees lose their leaves because keeping them with so few hours of sunshine in the winter isn't viable. But the leaves are made in such a way that they increase the drag effect. In many cases, they're even designed to spiral in a helix as they fall, making sure they will land close to the tree and preserve their nutrients. Basically, trees are good at everything.

It's true: a tree is a seat of learning from which we can explain the world.

What word would I use to say: "Each summer, I wake up every morning worried about forest fires"? If there's no name for something, does it really exist?

Etymologies bring us closer to what we once were, what we used to tell ourselves when things were different. Neologisms, on the other hand, give us insight into what we need to say, they help us invent ourselves. There's no lexicon for ecological disasters, the anxiety they provoke in us has no words. I read Glenn Albrecht and find the following terms:

"Anthropocene," coined by geologists to characterize the era dominated by humans.

"Capitalocene," the state of the planet in the wake of concepts such as colonialism, industrialization, globalization, racism, patriarchy. The place from which we can write our future as a species.

"Solastalgia," from the Latin, *solacium*, comfort, and *algos*, pain. Distress caused by climate change. Feeling that your home is crumbling around you.

"Symbiocene," the idea that we can integrate with other living things, understanding that life is interconnected, from what lives in our intestines up to huge ecosystems. Love for life and nature.

"Mermerosity," mourning felt in advance for species that are going to become extinct.

Whether these neologisms take hold or not, they show the need for words that allow us to share what is happening to us, that help us to recognize and think through the situation.

Naming is also a survival strategy.

And yet, not even fire puts an end to nature's dogged onward march.

Chernobyl.

The incredibly devastating effects of which, even thirty years later, we barely know the consequences. And the miracle of the plants that found a way of adapting to apparently impossible conditions.

In Chernobyl, the absence of humans has created a nature reserve, and animals have returned, even brown bears, which had not been seen there for over a century. Immediately after the disaster the plants were red and now they are an enthusiastic green; there are black poplars on roofs, birch trees on terraces; the asphalt, cracked open by bushes; avenues look like a green river. It's also true that radioactive matter captured by the vegetation is held inside it. What would happen if a fire burnt these forests down?

Within us, tragedy and pain are burning. Immemorial forests.

Forests also house fairy tale characters. That's where their parents abandon them, where they undergo a trial, from where they reemerge brave and transformed, ready to conquer a kingdom. For them, the forest is the symbol of life, as also for Oedipus who, after being rejected by his father, finds a new family in the forest. This tangle of plant life is the proving ground, the terrain that will endow us with bravery or in which we'll be devoured by the wolf.

Snow White took refuge from her wicked stepmother's envy in a hut in the forest. Also in the forest was the little gingerbread house belonging to the witch from Hansel and Gretel. A place of horror and also of fertility, the leafy forest allows one to remain hidden, and subsist, to undergo unexpected adventures; where it's possible to find food but also to perish.

After the Garden of Eden and its generative power, our ancestral memory holds the deep, dark forest. Some time ago we took shelter there, in that labyrinth of trees where, like lost children, we have to find our way out. The forest is the place of myth and also of philosophy.

"In some mysterious way woods have never seemed to me to be static things. In physical terms, I move through them; yet in metaphysical ones, they seem to move through me."[17]

Like columns of a temple or trees in a wood, things that rise produce spiritual tension, their verticality elevates us while what is horizontal brings us closer to death. Tension, silences, atmospheres, shaded paths, shushing leaves and their lingering smell, life teems in the trees and beneath them; under the trees we become contemplative, aspiring to something we could call "sacred."

Baudelaire rendered this image poetically in "Correspondences," his cornerstone of Symbolism. "Nature's a temple where each living column, / At times, gives forth vague words. There man advances / Through forest-groves of symbols, strange and solemn, / Who follow him with their familiar glances."[18]

Literature is seeded with images that we understand intuitively: to ascend is always to achieve something, to descend is to be rejected. One ascends to the throne, descends to the dungeon, rises to fame, and goes down to hell. Anabasis and katabasis. The way *ad inferos*, that stroll through the underworld that we've already encountered in the *Odyssey* and which finds its culmination in *The Divine Comedy*. And Rimbaud whispers: *A Season in Hell*.

When I write I don't need to explain, it's enough just to choose a space that will contain the idea; above or below, freedom or confinement, the place is part of the story, something

17 | John Fowles, *The Tree*.

18 | Charles Baudelaire, "Correspondences," trans. Roy Campbell.

that strikes a chord within us. What would *Wuthering Heights* be without its landscape?

Perhaps the columns of a temple are an imitation of a forest.

With my two little girls I rent a house in a village that is miraculous: mountains, a lake, the river, crystal streams, woods, and stone buildings; and all so close to Madrid. On Fridays, as soon as I leave work, we pick up the girls and the bus takes us to the Sierra Pobre. The house is tiny and has no garden, it's freezing in winter. Vegetable patches and fruit trees rub shoulders with houses, there are cows in the street, an ancient world inside another world that isn't quite modern. Sometimes there's a traveling theater company, or an improvised open-air cinema marked out with sheets. Sometimes, too, at the little crossroads, the town crier plays her bugle to announce the news, her strident tones blending with the afternoon's, adorned with birds.

If it's hot, we go down to the river. We take turns stretching out on a stone bed, the water—swift—cuts and baptizes. It's a beautiful, rugged spot, miniature yet grandiose. I can't put a name to the plants or birds, I'm an illiterate of the landscape. We trap tadpoles in pools so the girls can follow their amphibian journey, with eyes like periscopes; when their extremities appear, we return them to the river. Although we cast spells on them, none of the frogs become princes.

Teaching the girls how life begins. Telling stories, trying to transmit.

We go for great long walks around a shimmering brown lake; we don't have a car, so everything happens on foot. I ask my neighbor if she'll look after the youngest for a bit so that in the afternoons I can finally get down to some writing. She takes her out to the meadow with the cows and our house is filled with new words. Mine, on paper, and my daughter's words to describe a natural world which is unknown to me. When I see them setting off hand in hand, following the animals, I realize my daughters already belong to another world. One day the water disappears. The cracked dry earth reveals polished tree trunks, the remains of a submerged village. Ghosts.

I don't understand what it's all about until someone explains it to me. The persistent postwar drought. Franco and the reservoirs. Some things are erased from sight, but not from memory. I talk to people, they tell me stories of displaced families. In some villages, I'm told, even the dead were drowned.

What is not said, or touched upon, or even mentioned.

I've come to a country that denies the past.

So cold.

One summer I needed money, and it seemed like a good idea to enter a love letter writing competition with a piece I wrote about a fly, a farewell, to be more precise, because swatting tends to be definitive. I won, and since one of the conditions attached to winning the prize was going in person to receive it, I traveled to the town in La Mancha where it was organized. Heat and beach shoes. A straight line on the horizon, nostalgic, like in the pampa.

I was expecting a simple ceremony, but I was met with a hall brimming with people and television cameras, a podium with flowers, and, with my letter in hand, the threat of imminent and spectacular ridicule. The runners-up turned out to be a retired military man and a woman with a hair salon coif who disappeared into the toilet and reemerged dressed to the nines. Glitz. Military gait. Fierce gesture. For years, these runners-up had been crossing paths and brandishing text after text, piercing one another with wounding metaphors, scattering hatred born of failure, sonnets with triumphant rhymes, stories with not-so-happy-endings: they were battle-hardened professionals on the competition circuit.

The reading began. The runners-up let forth a stream of adjectives and subclauses that formed puddles in the room. And there I was, so ridiculous, with my fly and my beach shoes. Monterroso wrote: "There are three themes: love, death and flies."[19] Is there poetry without flies? "You, the familiar, / inevitable gluttons."[20]

And so, in a somewhat volatile way, writing started becoming inevitable for me.

I'm not the one who writes, it's somebody who inhabits me. I'm the one who bathes my daughters, soaks chickpeas, thinks up jam recipes. The one who works, reads and talks to friends, listens to her sisters, the one that's always tired. Inside me there's another woman who doesn't want to sleep and writes till dawn; waiting for the first birdcall to close her notebook and rest. That one who isn't me imagines and prunes texts until there's nothing left, journeys back to the seed of the idea, is surprised by her own insights, dances to the rhythm of words. That one who isn't me airs and tenderizes phrases, leaves them to soak, looks for fertile structures in which to sow stories. The other woman is the one who prunes plants and learns their Latin names, pores over seed catalogs, and is

19 | Augusto Monterroso, *Movimiento perpetuo* [Perpetual Motion], excerpt trans. Fiona Mackintosh.

20 | Antonio Machado, "Las moscas" [The Flies], excerpt trans. Fiona Mackintosh.

disorganized. The woman who writes, however, is demanding, rereads in bed, crosses out, and understands that, yet again, she hasn't quite managed it. The domestic self does jigsaws. The one who writes fits together the pieces of a life where there's never enough time for me.

Writing is like planting a garden.

I write short texts. I read.
Wisława Szymborska:
"When I pronounce the word silence,
I destroy it."[21]

A silent text is like a Japanese garden, a masterpiece of ellipses that invite meditative contemplation, where the visitor fills in the gaps. Condensing the essence. And imagination, unbound, runs free. Perhaps silence is at the core of all true art, the way of abstraction, minimalism, simplicity. Amidst the clamor of collective ceremonies, silence has become a luxury. You read in silence. You write in silence. In silence you can think.

It's nighttime and all is calm.

The world is mine.

On considering pruning as one of the fine arts:

I finish a story, revise it, half is left. I'm doing well. I prune everything that can be pruned; I become disenchanted with decorative ideas, I go beyond myself. The best adjective is a good noun. I let ideas emerge without naming them. I'd like to be read, as Lispector wanted, in the blank spaces.

I jot down an idea from Chekhov: the art of writing is the art of erasing.

21 | Wisława Szymborska, "The Three Oddest Words," trans. Clare Cavanagh and Stanisław Barańczak.

Less is more.

Clippings: once the pruning is done, trimmings of stories are left on the table. It causes me a pang to let them go, so I plant them as cuttings in tiny pots. To write is to approach and retreat at the same time. Watering and uprooting narcissism. Maybe one of these cuttings, like in the tale of the magic beans, will grow as high as the clouds and become a book.

Fertilizing: I avoid artificial fertilizer; instead I make compost with my own experiences, my own reading. Once the text has been fed, I let it rest; a certain distance allows the nutrients to sink in.

Culture, from the Latin "cultivation, cultivated."

To be cultivated. As if we were an orchard, or a garden.

A cultured person never stops growing.

There's an Arabic proverb that says: "A book is a garden that is carried in your pocket."

Time passes, and another, slightly bigger house will come along, a ruin: this time we'll be able to buy it. It's in a village close to Sigüenza with about two hundred inhabitants, mostly elderly.

I'm the first foreigner in the village's history, and the little square that my window looks out upon will become known as "la plaza de la argentina," the Argentinian woman's *plaza*. In renovating the building I retain its structure and style, and this surprises the builder; my foreign city-dweller's vision is conservationist, his wants to escape the past. After demolishing a former stable, we restore a tiny garden. Beside the wall there's a tuff stone that we can use for planting a rockery. It's the first time I've been able to sow seeds in the ground and, since I have more enthusiasm than space, I buy plants which I distribute around the village with no other intent than that of seeing them grow. But the neighbors look on suspiciously. For them, planting isn't giving away, it's taking over.

The tiny and the vast, the human desire to control, to manage the proportions of the world. Everything in the garden happens in miniature: memories, bushes, compost. I pile up clematis leaves to make compost. It's chalky terrain which makes choosing plants complicated: my dogwoods fail to thrive, but the lilacs are giddy with scent. I let the spirea petals fall like snow and realize that a rhododendron would be impossible. I'm learning a language; phosphorus, nitrogen, acidity, blight. It pains me not to know anything about chemistry, my scientific knowledge is mutilated.

I behave like an Agatha Christie character; at night I drop off to sleep while browsing plant catalogs, the water sing-songs along irrigation channels. My neighbor looks at them irritably and, shaking his head, says to me: "A tiny teardrop hardly falls before the sun drinks it up."

The countryside and its metaphors.

As the girls grow up and we blunder our way through fixing up the house, books—blithely ignoring my lack of time—emerge and start sprouting. I put up my defenses, try to avoid them, but I'm already writing a novel.[22] During the winter I give classes, I write in fertile gaps, I go to bed at daybreak. In the summer I have more time, vacations just mean a change of activity. So while I bring up my daughters, books, workshops, and houses come and go. Like one possessed, I work for over four years on each project, far away from and outside myself. I research, using external sources; I delve into things

22 | Clara Obligado, *La hija de Marx* [Marx's Daughter].

I'm ignorant about, writing is my way of thinking about the world. They say you should stick to what you know, but was Homer in Troy? My youngest climbs into bed with me and I tell her stories. I ask her if she knows what metamorphosis is. She thinks about it and replies: "A kind of camouflage." She's scared of heights, but she gets over it and jumps. She looks triumphantly at me and says: "I dizzified myself."

Words grow with my daughters.

I decide to go on a fact-finding mission for my novel. London and its squares, its balconies with window boxes; the wisdom of window-gardening. I want to research Marx's era, lose myself in the fabulous clothing collection of the Victoria and Albert Museum, to get ahold of Victorian erotica.

There is no section for erotica in the bookshops, but a beautiful *Kama Sutra* is displayed on the "beauty and health-care" shelves. I go into a porn shop and come face-to-face with a section on gardening books, and instead of a dildo I buy a plant. At the entrance to the V&A, a policeman who looks like a contract killer stops me, looks suspiciously at the package; I have visions of myself with my hands against the wall, prison, my family far away. But when he sees the plant, he relaxes, gives it a sniff, and grins: "What a lovely idea."

On the underground, in a section where the trains run almost at ground level, alongside the rails, I discover a miniature garden. Strictly speaking, it isn't really a garden, given its size and function; it's planted in a triangle where a single ray of sunlight breaks through, it mostly grows in the shadows, in the grime and polluted air. The man who designed it spends long hours below ground, but he has planted a garden that is touching, that expresses feeling and loneliness. What's curious about this tiny space in the midst of the hustle and bustle is the person who tends it, his courage. He has found time to water it, to press the earth down around the necks of the bulbs, to remove shriveled leaves. His efforts reveal his need to cling to a relationship with the earth that arose in Neolithic times, when people began tilling the land. Just as he needs work or food, this man needs beauty. Perhaps he has a makeshift, tedious, unfriendly job, but his garden gives him breathing space. Among the commuters fearful of clocking in late, among the faceless passengers, the switchman's fluttering garden is a model of resistance.

I go for long walks through the city, which, like Buenos Aires, is flat; how tiring are the slopes of the seven hills Madrid is built on. Windows show off the insides of houses. Spying on other people's lives without any consequences, weaving stories. I easily lose my sense of direction, to walk is to get lost, which is both a joy and a source of anxiety. The city as a jungle, as a wood with no trail of crumbs to show me the way.

A walk isn't the same as a pilgrimage.

I do remember my pilgrimages, hearts beating to a shared rhythm, with the Mothers of the Plaza de Mayo walking in a circle, crowds fighting for their rights. We women undertake a pilgrimage every March 8; those who set off on the Camino de Santiago are pilgrims. Pilgrimages bring together the physical and the spiritual, the head to the feet, the journey to the utopia.

Nevertheless, although time passes, there are echoes that never fall completely silent; they resound in unexpected places. I can't situate what I'm writing in the country I'm in, or in the country I left behind; to paint a territory opens up a wound in time and space that I don't want to confront. Space as a problem, the inability to build a nest. Displaced texts question the places where they're set, and in them the sense of loss leaves a powerful mark in the writing.

My sense of time is also disrupted, it stops being linear, it doesn't flow peacefully from one point to the next, but instead takes more daring shapes, spirals, jumps backwards or leaps forwards, meanders. It requires drilling down through the earth's crust to construct a new identity. I begin a project: it's set in an unspecified city brought to a standstill by garbage. Margins, dregs, waste.

When I arrived in Spain, I saw that people would throw a working washing machine in the dump, fridges just a few years old, beautiful furniture, perfectly wearable clothes. So much food.

What is trash?

"Trash" is not a universal concept, it depends on the society and its wealth, on the acceleration of capitalism. It's also what we sweep away under the carpet, what we don't like seeing. There's material trash, and also spiritual. There are human beings considered trash.

I jot down an idea: anyone looking for truth has to behave like someone who is digging through trash.

With the same energy with which I'd gone fact-finding in London, I flung myself into visiting garbage dumps. Everything was curiously shrouded in mystery: recycling plants were off limits, anonymous beings who sorted and separated glass, cardboard, plastics. A dystopian world.

In La Coruña there was an explosion at a dump: the build-up of gases flung all the garbage into the air and a man who happened to be walking there (walking *there*?), disappeared. Among the detritus, I saw his widow with a wreath. Over the white brows of foam, the environmentalists had spread a net to contain the mountains of garbage galloping toward the waves. Flocks of storks, frenzied seagulls squawking in circles. Beyond the closed garbage dump, the indifference of garbage trucks that carried on dumping from their sinister mouths.

Stench, reek, pestilence? It's impossible to describe, the smell of trash gets stuck in your nose. Very close by, the master recyclers, a Roma settlement, vital workers who no one wants to see. They go behind the fences to seek their spoils; they know the dump better than anyone, they change the meaning of objects.

The identity of things in the garbage dump mutates. A plate on a table is an object used in the eating process. Whereas if found in the dump, it can be a saint's halo, a flowerpot base or the discus flung by Myron's *Discobolus*. Things that are out of place, the odd one of a pair or series, become fantastic objects.

I go up and talk to the Romani.

"Once we reported finding a body and the police suspected us. Now, if we see something, we just leave it. Anyway, after a few days, there'll only be a belt left." She's a woman in her mid-thirties, already a grandmother. A girl walks past. Her shoes don't match. The impossible symmetry of the garbage dump. My character.

Beyond these borders, countries are converted into garbage dumps so that the ecological developed world, where all is sweetness and light, can keep its waste at arm's length. Galactic trash, spatial dumping grounds. Philosophers who talk about waste. A whole world.

I start writing.

The novel is called *Garbage*, but the editor sees my proposal, gives me a look and says with irony, "Yeah, right."[23]

When I finish the project, I have spent almost four years thinking about it and it's really beginning to get me down.

23 | Clara Obligado, *Si un hombre vivo te hace llorar* [If a Living Man Makes You Cry].

Now everything makes me feel guilty, I separate and sort obsessively. Instead of changing the world with my novel, the novel is changing me; I see things I didn't previously want to see, I see my life from a different angle.

My house is only habitable because I get rid of all surplus, I refuse responsibility for it and, with hardly a glance at the trash can, I stretch out my hand. If we had to live around everything we throw away and glimpsed the sheer magnitude of our indifference, we'd be aware of the problem. But garbage dumps are far away; in rich neighborhoods, trash cans are hidden in the basement. Meanwhile garbage trucks drive off with their loads squashed into black bags. I understand where the money is in this putrid circle: in transport. Garbage is a business that stinks.

I've gotten myself a home compost bin to dispose of my vegetable peelings, and my life expands to include leachates and worms. Tangles of worms like the Gorgons' hair, miniature excavators, writhing invertebrates that digest organic waste and turn it into compost. Although individual action is absurd, I dream of a garden that can give back to the earth all that comes from it. Am I pitting writing against destruction? At the very least, I'm fighting against my own paralyzing pessimism.

My book is also looking for its family, its natural affinities. Who can I dialogue with? What do I belong to, if I have neither generation nor country? Where are my peers? A friend recommends a novel on the subject, *Bariloche*, written by a very young Argentinian writer also living in Spain. Is it a coincidence? I don't think so. I write to him and we meet up. The years go by and I begin to think of Andrés Neuman as part of my generation, not because of his age—he could be my son—but because of shared experiences and interests; there's something we have in common without needing to explain.

I can't help comparing writing to nature, my literary strategies increasingly converge with nature's ways, she presides over a model economy, everything is reused and whatever dies becomes fertilizer. The tension of texts, that primordial need for contact and words. I think these things and, through the window, observe the moon.

According to the giant-impact hypothesis, the moon was born out of a huge collision between a protoplanet and ours that took place four thousand million years ago, formed with debris from the impact. What would the Earth be without the moon? How many sentimental poems would we have been spared? The ancients called her Selene, one of the Titanesses; she belongs to the deities who ruled the earth in the Golden Age, when there were no wars, work, old age, or infirmity, and we died placidly, as if in a dream.

The moon gradually moves away from us and for centuries she hid half her face. Imagine those days, when every night held that mystery; we are so prone to projecting our feelings onto the indifferent cosmos. Losing sight of her is a matter of time, I sometimes tell myself, and in that lingering transit unfolds all the intelligence of the world. Nature isn't endangered, we are; the wisest strategy would be to join forces with her.

Nor will books disappear, they germinate ideas that will slowly emigrate. There's a literary garden, a wood we stroll through, where each species resonates. Analogies between art and nature are endless, no era has failed to evoke them.

Little by little, I stop contemplating the world as something separate and other, and understand that the world looks upon me with indifference; I'm part of a species that is one small part of the planet's story, and I can disappear without anything much changing. Why do we place ourselves in the center of creation? Even without humans, another hundred million years of planetary exuberance spurred on by the sun could carry life beyond the Earth. And this certainty, which goes beyond me and terrifies me, also fills me with a stubborn, abstract kind of hope.

I look at the moon again and feel it's backwards, that it's waxing and waning in the opposite direction. Not even the moon stays in place when you change hemisphere.

I always read in bed until the early hours. My neighbor sees the bedroom light on, and is also late to bed because he runs the only bar in the village. I read, in Mary Oliver's *Upstream*, a chapter entitled "The Owl's Cry."

Recently I've managed to keep slightly more regular hours; I turn the light off at three in the morning. I feel happy at this minor triumph, and allow the night to flow.

Spring is humid. A huge moon illuminates the balcony. The owl from the book flies over a wood where buds swell on trees and the broom is in flower, yellow brushstrokes across the still-snowcapped mountains.

I like owls. They are the emblem of wise Pallas Athene, and companions of Merlin. Owls are also revered in my homeland, they teach you to look back before taking flight. The owl from the book is hungry and hunts in this world I inhabit. At the foot of my bed, the cat is drowsily purring; suddenly he becomes alert and looks out the window, but then closes his eyes again. If he was in the story I'm reading, my cat might lose his life in the owl's grip, a chase, a bloodcurdling yowl, the bird's talons plunged into his back. Nature is not in the least kind; we like projecting our feelings onto her.

I sleep among wingbeats and bloodthirstiness; the bird's unblinking yellow eyes examine me. In the morning,

I go down to my neighbor's bar for breakfast. "Did you see the owl?" he asks me. "It was perched on the railings of your balcony. It's rare to see an eagle owl around here. Did you hear its cry?"

I'm convinced the book came to life as a bird. As though Mary Oliver conjured it up. As if my reading wasn't real, but a reflection of the night. I also think about how books give light in darkness.

"Animal," from the Latin, *animal, animalis*. Animate, having a soul. The breath of life that unites us.

I invite Papá to visit the plot of land I bought in La Vera; he likes this kind of project and, since he's quite elderly, I plan the journey carefully; I don't know whether he'll make it to Spain again. Since he can hardly walk anymore, I take a folding chair in the car and also some insect repellent for his papery skin. I ask him to come up with a scheme for the plot of land, he can read all the signs in the landscape. Someday, I tell him, we'll build a house here, and this will be the garden.

"If you're going to plant trees," he says, "Make sure they're fruit trees. They're pretty, and they give you food. I wish I hadn't planted so many decorative trees."

The plot is outlandish and beautiful, I got it for next to nothing when people weren't into such harebrained schemes. There are two old, ruined tobacco-drying sheds, a valley, and a little oak wood, the silvery thread of a river. In the distance, snowy mountains. Willows grow here, quite a rarity since people stopped basket-weaving; there are brambles and broom on the slopes, a horse chestnut the height of a cathedral, and terraced hills where sweet peppers were planted, now crumbling away.

Too much for a garden, not enough for setting up a business.

I just love ruins. Restoring the essence of things, seeing the soul of a house, putting it back on its feet, letting it express itself. I'd never live in a house without ghosts.

While the others are exploring the piece of land, I sit down with Papá beside the river, under the oak trees, and we chat quietly. He's still got his sense of humor, his almost childlike wonder.

"I've been thinking," he says suddenly. "I know just what you need."

I wait for my father's suggestions. His wisdom.

"You should bring two pregnant cows from Buenos Aires."

"Two cows?"

I presume it's a joke, but he insists, explains, rambles.

"Yes. Two Jersey cows, they're docile, easy to transport, give good milk. They'd make it here alright." And he repeats: "Pregnant."

Suddenly I realize that I've already lost him.

We don't make it. We never make it on time. Those of us who live far away, in the other hemisphere, if the agony isn't long, we never arrive on time to accompany our loved ones in death. It's our curse: a call in the night and the sudden cry, the definitive cut, someone who over there, in *our* world, has gone forever. Then the shadows close in. Their curse, their blessing. I read Tanizaki and am comforted by his homespun philosophy, his song to the darkness. What is lost and sinks. Its forlorn beauty. And writing that captures nuances, preserves miniscule details, sheds light on them again.

It's early, the palm tree is drawing its shadows on the wall. When we moved into this house it only had three fronds, like the tufts of a dying bird. We had to prune several trees to let the light in and now its wild mane explodes beside the window. I hear its swishing, its fanned shadow falls on the patio. Garden light, dappled gold between midday branches, pink fading to gray at twilight, that half-dark which carries me over to the stimulus of night, my writing time. Goethe wrote: "What is hardest of all? / That which seems most simple: to see with your eyes / what is before your eyes."

I imagine darkness as a freed land.

I imagine my father, who I will never see again.

"Somber." "Umbra." "Sombrous." "Sombrero." "Umbrella."

"Cloud." "Becloud."

Word families. I read Corominas's *Etymological Dictionary* the way people read novels.

A shock, but also a delight: the ghosts of Papá and Mamá. Mamá died one night when I was still young, and so was she. My second daughter had just been born and, when I got the call, I started crying. I cried for the rest of the night, I cried as I phoned to say I wouldn't be going into work, I cried at the travel agent's where they gave me a free flight that I would later pay for, I cried on the plane. I cried as I carried my daughter in the airport, I cried as if I wanted to wash away the world. I cried in the cemetery (but that was more logical), I cried until I understood that it is more complicated to say goodbye to someone with whom you have a difficult relationship than to someone with whom everything has been easy.

I didn't make it to her burial, no one was there to comfort me. All the mourners were shut up in their own homes, caught up in their own grief. I slept in my father's house and that night, my daughter started crying too. I got out of bed to comfort her and saw my mother in her nightdress coming along the passageway. The scene was calm. To begin with, I was struck by her being there, because my parents had separated years before. But then I thought: she's come to say goodbye. And I smiled at her. Then, because I was naked, I felt embarrassed and went back to bed. Cradled by her image, I fell asleep.

My father, on the other hand, died several times. He had Alzheimer's, and every time I went to Buenos Aires, I would come back to Madrid feeling desperately sad, thinking I'd never see him again. They say Alzheimer's is a brutal disease, which it is, but it's also other things; in those last few years I had a relationship with my father in which as I got older, he was regressing toward childhood, and we both accepted that we'd communicate through touch. One day, seeing us three sisters together, he said: "What charming ladies, apparently they're my daughters."

As his life headed back toward its starting point, my father first became a surrealist poet, then he almost entirely stopped speaking Spanish and reverted to French, taking shelter in the language of his childhood, and eventually he curled up inside music. When they told me he was dying I decided not to travel, as he was no longer conscious, and the idea of going for a few days without knowing whether I could accompany him to the end was too painful. So he died, and I held him in my memory.

Those of us who are far away have to invent our own rituals for saying goodbye. My father had always been a *bon vivant*, so to remember him, our family ate at a restaurant he loved, and we toasted to him. We went to see a funny movie, the last one we'd seen together. At the time he was being buried, I went to mass, even though I'm not a believer; I accompanied him as he would have wanted, I know it would have pleased him. The mass was dedicated to Isidore the Farmer, the most fitting saint.

Coincidences, compensations.

Years went by. I was coming back from a journey when among those waiting to greet passengers, I glimpsed Papá's face. He wasn't ill anymore, and he must have been about my age; his agelessness and my stage of life had rendered us equal. So I told him: Papá, I'm older now and pretty happy. I'm still with my partner, I've won the odd prize or two, we've got a grandson who I wish you'd met. My daughters are fine. All five of your children are still working the land, in our different ways. You'd be happy. I miss you terribly.

And I walked away from the station, dragging my suitcase.

In the empty night; I walk alone. There'll never again be that house or that door; I don't know which is the last mirror he looked into, but I'll keep talking to him. The things in the house won't know they've gone, even though all that's left of my parents is a handful of earth.

When I go back to the countryside I'll also think: this is the tree my father planted, these are the curtains my mother chose. This is where the dog used to sleep peacefully. There was a jasmine bush and I wasn't happy. Here's where I learned to get lost in nature and take refuge in books. Here I was loved, and I learned to love.

Shadows emerge from their cave when I go back to the countryside. The formal park is erased by floods, mighty trees have extended their titanic branches. The walnut tree, like a motionless dome, suicides the brains of its fruits. We're still there, our child bodies, I'm hidden, away from prying adult eyes, I read surrounded by the brilliant yellow of the sweet acacia. Further on is where don Juan used to live, I hear the greyhounds bark, the odd horse whinny. I see us, my sister and me, hear distant shouting. I see blood on the ground. I see my mother being miserable.

Gentle rain waters the garden.

I'm raining.

What if we woke up one morning and, like Gregor Samsa, had turned into insects? Or into foxes, like in David Garnett's novel? Literature is full of metamorphoses. The gods of Olympus took on animal shapes to get up to their wily tricks, and their victims transformed themselves in order to hide; amphibians make us realize just how imprecise binary definitions can be.

I used to have a dog called Lúa, and she joined our household against my wishes. In Madrid you have to look out for female dogs, and I wasn't willing to, so I only accepted her on condition that someone else would keep an eye on her. That way, a deep love evolved between us, based entirely on pleasure and not on obligation. Lúa was a crossbreed, which meant she looked odd and her fur was unmanageable. When I took her to the countryside, she ran around the outside of the house whirling up dark leaves. There are few sights happier or more life-affirming than that of a dog running. When she got tired out, she'd clamber into my lap and hide her head under the giant wing of my arm. Then all of a sudden, she'd inexplicably start trembling. Lúa had a history. Maybe she'd been mistreated, perhaps her former life was cocooned inside her new life, or it was an ancestral fear. If she awoke, she'd look up at me trustingly before falling back asleep. A dog is a bunch of neuroses. Lúa always needed to be in contact with someone, have their hand on her head, be under my feet when I was writing, or underneath my bed at night. One day she stood on her hind legs and leaned against mine, quietly watching me. Suddenly, beneath her mop of curly fur, I saw my mother's gaze. They both had dark, watery eyes, which readily communicated how they were feeling. This version of my mother in front of me was calm and affectionate, in a way she'd never been. Or had she? Perhaps something of her was there to comfort me, in my living room, where a little dog and I were gazing into each other's eyes. Then Lúa lowered herself back down, shook her ears, and crawled under the table. I never saw Mamá again.

In Hiroshima, there are trees that survived the atomic bomb. The Japanese call them *hibakujumoku*, and they are a hymn to the enduring power of life. These wise ancients are known and respected: a ginkgo, a black Japanese pine with a scar, and a muku, three species commonly found in traditional gardens. There's also a weeping willow, sprung from roots that had survived below ground 370 meters away from the catastrophe. The ginkgo sprouted among the ruins of an old Buddhist temple and is now the symbol of rebirth. Someone wrote beneath it: "Never again Hiroshima."

I'm going to buy a ginkgo. I won't live long enough to sit under its fan-shaped leaves, but planting a tree is always an act of hope. I plant the ginkgo and remember that this tiny fragile-looking tree came into the world before the arrival of the dinosaurs. It has no living relatives, it is the only member of its genus. Over the years, its growth doesn't slacken off and the quality of its seeds doesn't diminish with age. It may die due to some external cause, but unlike me, it doesn't carry its death within it. As the poet José Martí said: "Plant a tree, have a child, write a book."[24] Leave a trace of our passing through the world. Transcend. My father believed there was a heaven. I worship the kingdom of this world. When I turned sixty, I decided it was

24 | Editor's note: this proverb is commonly translated from the Spanish: "Plantar un árbol, tener un hijo, escribir un libro."

time to start growing old, but I put it off. Now I'm over seventy and I've put it off again. While I laugh at my own survival strategies, I imagine the trees and their triumph over time. I fantasize about those to come, my grandson's grandchildren, who might enjoy the breeze beneath these branches. I write this book and gently plant the ginkgo; to cultivate a tree is to let myself be cultivated by it.

Wholeness and fragments, great and small: nature, landscape, garden, herbarium.

Settings, cuttings.

I try to define these words. Nature is a unified whole, unlimited. Landscape, in contrast, is torn off, it's a fragment; mankind's gaze individualizes it, separates it, though this fragment is in tune with the whole and shares a common feeling. Georg Simmel expresses this, in his *Philosophy of Landscape.* Gardens, on the other hand, are smaller spaces where we like to imagine that nature expresses itself, when in reality, it's quite the opposite. A garden is nature manipulated: we "compose" harmonious borders, we uproot "weeds," we prize a fashionable hybrid, we prune bushes into novel shapes, we mercilessly exterminate any "blight" bold enough to live among our flowers. What would happen to a poor serpent if it dared to rear its head in our paradise?

While I tend my garden, I muse that we all have several lives not lived. In one I dreamed of being a Victorian painter who sketched flowers with obsessive precision and the sweetness of jam.

I enjoy drawing, I amass notebooks where I jot things down for my books and sketch scenes that mean something only to me, but help me remember details: the pistol to be used by the murderer, the palm tree that will sway beside the balcony, a corner of the room where I'm writing. After I've finished one of my clumsy drawings I know how the petals of a gardenia fold or what a fly's wings are like, and that precision has something to do with searching for the *mot juste*.

People often approach nature meticulously and microscopically, taking it as a challenge of classification. "No one has arranged the different groupings of nature in such a perfect order," said Linnaeus—without undue modesty—about himself.[25]

I think of Rosa Luxemburg and her herbarium comprising eighteen notebooks. She organized some of them when she was in prison, as if she sought to caress with her hands the life that was going on in the outside world. Later, her murdered body was recovered from the river, and she lay anonymously in the catacombs of the Charité Hospital in Berlin for ninety-one years until saliva was extracted from the herbarium to match with her DNA, and she finally received a proper burial.

Making an herbarium is a vain attempt to triumph over the chaos of nature, establish order and observe things separately. It's also the vain and foolish attempt to classify everything. I think about what escapes us, the comfort that small things give us. About letting ourselves go with the flow. About chaos.

The word "chaos" has an Indo-European root that is associated with both "gas" and "yawning." In Greek it designates a dark abyss produced at the dawn of time, which in Greek philosophy and cosmogony means "formless matter." Chaos existed before the creation of the world, and from it came Nyx, night, Erebus, darkness, and Gaia, the earth.

25 | Editor's note: this quote, widely attributed to Linnaeus, was translated by Fiona Mackintosh.

So it's a yawn and a beginning. I like the idea that the creative impulse germinates between laziness and disorder.

Houses. The histories they harbor. Hospitality. Places that will take you in, a guest room, food that multiplies, like in the miracle of the loaves and fishes.

In a little-known tragedy by Euripides, Alcestis has to undertake a journey to Hades. Or to put it in more current language, she has died and must travel to the great beyond. Her husband, [Admetus], laments her loss and, in the midst of mourning, receives an untimely visit from Hercules. Hercules is unaware of his host's pain as, in order not to burden the demigod, [Admetus] hides his suffering. When Hercules finds out how generous his host has been, he in turn bestows a gift, which consists of bringing back his wife, [Alcestis], from the shades of death. A tragedy with a happy ending. We're all at one time or another guests or hosts; we protect and accept protection.

"I went to the woods because I wished to live deliberately, to front only the essential facts of life, and see if I could not learn what it had to teach, and not, when I came to die, discover that I had not lived."

Thoreau's decision to withdraw to a small cabin in the woods is well known. There he writes *Walden*, a beautiful book in which he proposes a series of maxims that help to change the world with the not-so-simple system of changing oneself. Simplicity, austerity, rurality, frugality are the cardinal virtues. "The art of doing without" in which Thoreau discovers that he can survive on only six weeks of manual labor a year.

"I had three chairs in my house; one for solitude, two for friendship, three for society. When visitors came in larger and unexpected numbers [. . .] they generally economized the room by standing up. [. . .] My 'best' room, however, my withdrawing room, [. . .] was the pine wood behind my house."

Thoreau's chairs give much food for thought. In some villages, if there are two people, there are two seats; in others it's inconceivable to have a house without a comfortable bed for travelers.

There is another beautiful and less well-known book, written by Susan Fenimore Cooper (1813–1894), who, six years before Thoreau, wrote the founding text of environmentalism, *Journal of a Naturalist.* Her approach is less stiff. Darwin said: "I am in the middle of Miss Cooper's 'Journal of a Naturalist.' Who is she? She seems a very clever woman and gives a capital account of the battle between our and your weeds." The book came out anonymously, and Susan Fenimore Cooper, daughter of the author of *The Last of the Mohicans*, published it signed "By a lady."

Between their two woodland cabins, I would have preferred arriving at Susan's, since, as well as offering me a seat, she'd have greeted me, doubtless, with some of her homemade cake. Being forgotten is part of women's history.

I start thinking about this book. About preserving on paper that slice of nature that became writing. I think about telling things in a disorderly fashion, like someone going for a stroll, joining the verdant dots. I jot down anecdotes to see whether they'll flower. I feed them and the shade of a tree rises up.

Everything I see infiltrates what I write.

What comes into my head is the planet's daily orbit, its survival strategies, that slow pace so different from ours, the clouds that gather and disperse, our enlightened human attitude that turns its back on the landscape. When I say "landscape" I'm not talking about tamed nature, but about the environment, our *oikos*, this neglected home.

I plant, filled with hope, the first few phrases and the text expands in fractals, stories unfold like the branches of an ash tree, I structure the stories in logarithmic spirals, I interweave and train their shoots. It nearly always works. Just looking at the veins of a leaf is enough to come up with the outline of a story. Logarithmic spirals evoke perfection, and are replicated in the world at large: the turns of the Milky Way, the head of a sunflower, birds in flight. It's also the golden ratio of the Renaissance. Why are we moved by it? Why are we bewitched by a flower or a landscape? What do we project onto them, that makes us feel so deeply?

Some people thought nature was a reflection of the divine, others, of what we carry in our hearts, others saw it as a hostile medium that had to be subjugated; history and art have mulled these concepts over endlessly. Perhaps it's the memory of what we were, our passage through different species, maybe it's something we can't narrate, just as it's impossible to "tell the story" of a Bach fugue; what happens inside us when we hear it is beyond, or before, words.

But for those of us who write, of course, we need words for naming.

This summer I'm going to finish writing some short stories in a house in the middle of France that a friend has loaned us. There's a garden I look after for her, and a cat who stalks me, looking neurotic. I try to win him over with extra food, but still, he hates me; he makes it quite clear that he's the master of the house and I'm the intruder. I forget him while I'm out walking through the fields and delicious little woods, the villages full of flowers. From the bedroom window Chartres cathedral is visible, like a cardboard cut-out. I write, and in my free time, decide to visit the local gardens.

The first one I come across is tiny; the owner presents it as a medieval garden and he trails along behind us, trying to sell us soap and postcards. It's rather unkempt, but that neglect is precisely what makes it appealing. It models itself on the Garden of Eden and can be interpreted on two levels: water represents eternal life, and the plants all carry a symbolic meaning. Its checkerboard layout is a nourishing and healing space, with fruits, spices, and a medicinal herb garden. Beneath the vines, which evoke both wine and the Eucharist, the shade is a spiritual walk, with a wall separating us from the fearful outside world. What a restful life.

We come to Maintenon, where there's a palace with a formal garden designed by André Le Nôtre. Le Nôtre was a gardener and painter, therefore a master of the art of perspective, which created much admiration in the early seventeenth century. In his gardens, which are the highest example of formal French gardens, vistas stretch off to infinity: straight avenues, sculpted parterres, bordered ponds, fountains, obelisks, statuary. [Le Nôtre], as we know, designed that machine of vision from which you could see the dominion of the Sun King: the gardens at Versailles. The garden as power and its exhausting walkways. I sit down to contemplate the aqueduct that today resembles a romantic ruin. Measuring sticks in hand, the gardeners solicitously prune the hedge borders of the parterre to the perfect height. Gardens reflect the illusions of their era, meditation or prestige, intimacy or displays of power.

Following the river that Le Nôtre domesticated, we come to Giverny, where the painter Claude Monet devoted himself to a new creative outlet, that of gardening. Vegetation, watery mirrors, even a Japanese bridge were part of his perfectionist passion, and the garden became an ever-changing painting, rich in colors, hues, light, and shade. A twist on the idea that art imitates nature, suggesting that nature imitates art. What was not factored into its delicate design was the huge influx of tourists who nowadays invade its paths. Many of them pause at the waterlily pond, which caused the waters of the River Epte to be rerouted and filtered to produce an always clean, gentle stream. The garden's charm is undeniable, but there's something odd about this evidently "picturesque" nature, a term that spilled over from the field of art into philosophy and poetry, or the world of travel.

It's getting dark and I leave feeling overwhelmed. Strolling through the little town where the painter used to walk restores a spell that mutes the babble of the visitors.

Back in La Vera, we pick a melon that grew from the worm compost. We left it there the whole summer and it went on swelling up like a pregnant woman. Someone told us that when the stalk that comes out of its belly button has dried up, the melon will be fully ripe. We take it to Madrid, to share with everyone who'd been in the house over the summer. Everything has its rightful moment.

The garden at La Vera is tiny and orderly, I've planted samples there of all that grew in the countryside of my childhood. A silvery gray *Teucrium*, some *Agapanthus africanus* which give the tiny pool the look of a pond. Seeing them, I realize I'm recreating my childhood park in miniature. I compose the garden like someone recalling a lost word.

The plants of our childhood are unchanging. Like memories, they neither die nor grow.

Communicating vessels between writing and planting: a gardener's greatest asset is patience, not in the sense of passivity, but rather an insistence that feeds on surprises. Likewise, someone who writes is patient in their search, nothing fertilizes a text better than waiting.

That's how books grow.

In these uncertain times, as the pandemic seems to be abating, I remember the months that have passed since lockdown began. Remote working allowed me to fulfill a long-held ambition: to see the seasons change in nature, to live out a whole year in the countryside.

With my daughter we restore the tobacco-drying shed. It's a humble old building in the wood. Wild boars come up to the house and scratch their hides against the trees, leaving traces of mud and nighttime revelry on the bark. In the cottony fog, oak and ash lose their leaves then become green again. There's moss, bulbs, delicate wildflowers. It's a European deciduous forest so distant from the pampa where I spent part of my childhood, less elemental than that landscape, more scribbled over.

The year has been both long and short, full of pain and uncertainty. I have finished two short essays that complement one another, *Una casa lejos de casa*, in which I talked about exile, changing country, the heartache of emigrating. The one I'm writing now is like a mirror image, it reproduces the structure, and my other self expands its senses. Might I go on like this, in an endless loop? We all have multiple personalities, and some are practically incompatible. How does our inner writer express itself?

Once, in my workshop, talking about Borges, we decided to do the following exercise: we took one of his short stories, analyzed its sentence structures and, using them as scaffolding, we changed the meaning of the words; we engaged in a secret plagiarism that was very hard to spot, we replicated, feeding off the bones rather than the flesh. I find such experiments fascinating. To what extent are we ourselves when we write? What is it that unmistakably identifies us? Writing, I tell myself, is simultaneously lying and telling the truth. I write this and find myself wondering: Is truth a literary virtue?

I read Ana Casas's work, and dialogue with her. She says: "Creatives keep struggling to capture their identity, albeit in a partial and precarious way."[26] I ponder her words. I've never been interested in talking about myself, but a personal thread flows through and organizes me. Does it feed off the need to reflect that comes with age, or is it simply a technique for weaving together this discourse? Is it a hybrid accent? Is writing in the first person a strategy to avoid generalizing my reflections? Am I more sincere in my syntax, or in the stories I tell myself? Who knows. Rimbaud wrote: "Je est un autre," I is an other.[27] My "I"s are paths along which my stories walk.

As I write, it's raining. Not the kind of rain that gently waters the garden, it's the kind that lashes the ground furiously. "Rain is something that no doubt happens in the past,"[28] the poet says, and I let myself be dampened by his nostalgia. Today it's raining the way it used to in my childhood, but it no longer smells of ozone, it's different to rain in the pampa. Clouds roll in from the sea; the miracle of salt, which is heavy and can't evaporate or ascend to the clouds; the shape of raindrops. What shape is a raindrop? We might say it's like a tear. Is that because it's inescapably melancholy? No, the air shapes a raindrop, and it's shaped like a little hamburger bun.

Rain falls on the garden and the hydrangeas bow their

26 | Ana Casas, *El autor a escena: Intermedialidad y autoficción* [The Author on Stage: Intermediality and Autofiction].

27 | Arthur Rimbaud, "Lettre à Georges excerpt trans. Fiona Mackintosh. [Letter to Georges Izambard, May 13, 1871].

28 | Jorge Luis Borges, "La lluvia" [Rain], excerpt trans. Fiona Mackintosh.

pink heads; the cypress tree stops looking at the sky to droop low. It rains and as I write, a majestic clap of thunder ricochets off the mountain.

Words that I collect:

"Celaje," how the sky looks when it is streaked with faint clouds of different colors.

"Cencellada," beautiful and frozen, it defines an ice cloud.

"Ventalle," fanning. Saint John of the Cross wrote: "And the fanning of the cedars made a breeze."[29]

On pain and creation.

Crushed by his experience as chronicler of numerous humanitarian crises, the Brazilian photographer Sebastião Salgado abandoned Rwanda in order to photograph the earth. And thus *Genesis* was born, a book which aims to show the places in the world that remain unchanged since the day of creation. Then he returned to the land of his childhood, in Minas Gerais, to take over his father's farm. What he found was no longer the Eden of his childhood. The countryside, completely devastated, had become a dry and barren region. Together with his wife, Lélia Wanick, he vowed to restore the lost subtropical Atlantic forest to that land. The before and after images are moving. Where there was desert, now trees are growing, and water is flowing once more.

Wangari Muta Maathai, winner of the Nobel Peace Prize, urged the women of Kenya to gather seeds from the forests to plant them, and she managed to leave a legacy of more than forty million trees. There are many initiatives like this one that aren't an exercise in nostalgia but teach us instead that to live is to be reborn incessantly, like the cells of our bodies.

29 | Saint John of the Cross, "Dark Night of the Soul," trans. E. Allison Peers.

People also say that if a burnt forest is left to its own devices, ten years later it will regenerate.

There's a concept that I find stimulating, that of "de-extinction." It might not make much sense to revive a dinosaur whose habitat has disappeared, but there are more recently extinct animals that could be brought back. Aurochs, for example, a kind of wild cattle that used to clear the countryside and prevent wildfires. As auroch genes are present in various contemporary species of cattle, the method consists of crossing those animals closest to the original, and getting gradually closer with each generation. By the seventh generation, according to geneticists, you would see the extinct animal alive and kicking once more.

When everything seems to be falling apart, I read Steiner; I approach his books like someone sitting down next to a wise man for whom literature is a way of breathing. He also talks about resurrecting the past, about the classics and their vitality; I undertake a journey with him, to the origin; I see how language germinates. Syntax, morphology, what doesn't jump out at you but is there, grammar as a structure of human experience.

Steiner speaks of the future tense like a gift from the verb, a form that allows us to project ourselves toward imaginary universes. A verb tense, he says, which defies death and desperation, the time in which we can dream. He also says: "It's fantastic that we humans are animals that can conceive of futurity and have at our disposal a verb form to express it. If someone were to wrest that possibility from us, we would be bereft of the gift that has allowed us to survive horror, massacres, hunger."[30]

To live is to rewrite ourselves.

30 | George Steiner and Cécile Ladjali, *Eloge de la transmission: Le maître et l'élève* [In Praise of Transmission], excerpt trans. Fiona Mackintosh.

And the word was made time, it defied death and desperation.

My father taught me the importance of plants; I give my grandson the gift of a hyacinth bulb so he can see it sprout. I see his astonished little face and remember myself at his age, observing how a geranium's red flower peeps out. I explain to him what leachings are, I show him the labor of worms. I tell him that I chat with the palm tree peering in through the window. Bruno plants and listens to me, in his half-language he repeats names in Latin. As I did with my daughters, we play at learning tricky words. I know I don't have time to find out what he'll do with his life, so I try to pass on to him what might be useful. I'm a narrator, a link in a chain, a branch. He's digging with a stick, planting a seed. Will he remember me?

I tell him part of his family comes from far away and a chapter of the *Odyssey* comes to mind, that story of an impossible return, the ten years of war that turn the hero into a stranger. So when Odysseus returns home, only his dog recognizes him. His father doesn't know who he is, but wily Odysseus finds a private safe-conduct: "If you like, I can list for you all the trees you once gave to me in this well-kept orchard: since I, when I was a child, followed you and asked for them one by one; and, as we walked among them you showed them to me and told me their names. There were thirteen pear trees, ten apple trees, and forty figs; and you also offered me fifty rows of vines."

And his father, overcome, embraced him.

I evoke these stories that have been repeated since time immemorial, the topos of the returning hero. With less fanfare, we women also return to a nature that reminds us of its motherly essence.

Juan Ramón Jiménez said: "And I will go, and the birds

will remain, singing."[31]

What do I desire for my grandchildren? As I finish writing I make a wish: if some day they make a return journey, I hope to have shown them a path. Sitting next to Bruno, in the garden, in this very domestic way, I allow myself to inhabit that great error which is hope.

31 | Juan Ramón Jiménez, "The Final Voyage," trans. Paula Luteran.

SOURCES

Albrecht, Glenn. *Earth Emotions: New Words for a New World*. Ithaca, NY: Cornell University Press, 2019.

Alonso, Lina. "El herbario de Rosa Luxemburgo" [Rosa Luxemburg's Herbarium]. In *El Malpensante*, October 26, 2018.

Araújo, Joaquín. *Los árboles te enseñarán a ver el bosque* [The Trees Will Show You the Wood]. Prologue by Manuel Rivas. Barcelona: Crítica, 2020.

Baudelaire, Charles. "Correspondences." In *Poems of Baudelaire: Les Fleurs du Mal.* Translated by Roy Campbell. New York: Pantheon Books, 1952.

Benjamin, Walter. "Paris of the Second Empire in Baudelaire." In *The Writer of Modern Life: Essays on Charles Baudelaire*. Edited by Michael W. Jennings. Translated by Howard Eiland, Edmund Jephcott, Rodney Livingston, and Harry Zohn. Cambridge, MA: Belknap Press of Harvard University Press, 2006.

Berjman, Sonia. *Diversas maneras de mirar el paisaje* [Different Ways of Looking at Landscape]. Buenos Aires: Nobuko, 2005.

Beruete, Santiago. *Verdolatría. La naturaleza nos enseña a ser humanos* [Greenolatry: Nature Teaches Us to be Human]. Madrid: Turner Noema, 2018.

Blanchot, Maurice. "Literature and the Right to Death." In *The Gaze of Orpheus and Other Literary Essays*. Translated by Lydia Davis. Barrytown, NY: Station Hill Press, 1981.

Borges, Jorge Luis. "El Fin" [The End]. *La Nación* (Buenos Aires), 1953.

Borges, Jorge Luis. "La lluvia" [Rain]. In *El hacedor*. Buenos Aires: Emecé Editores, 1960.

Borges, Jorge Luis. "Posesión del ayer" [Possession of Yesterday]. In *Los Conjurados*. Madrid: Alianza Editorial, 1985.

Bourriaud, Nicolas. *The Radicant*. Translated by James Gussen and Lili Porten. London: Stemberg Press, 2009.

Brontë, Emily. *Wuthering Heights*. London: Thomas Cautley Newby, 1847.

Calvet, Louis-Jean . *Historias de las palabras* [Word Histories]. Spanish version by Soledad García Mouton. Madrid: Gredos, 1996.

Carson, Rachel. *Silent Spring.* Boston: Houghton Mifflin, 1962.

Carson, Rachel. *Lost Woods: The Discovered Writing of Rachel Carson*. Boston: Beacon Press, 1999.

Casas, Ana. *El autor a escena: Intermedialidad y autoficción* [The Author on Stage: Intermediality and Autofiction]. Madrid: Iberoamericana-Vervuert, 2017.

Castillo, Ramón del. *Filósofos de paseo* [Wandering Philosophers]. Madrid: Turner Noema, 2020.

Ceric, Teodor. *Jardins en temps de guerre* [Gardens in Wartime]. Arles: Actes Sud, 2014.

Clément, Gilles. *Manifeste du Tiers paysage* [Manifesto of the Third Landscape]. Bremen: Sujet Verlag, 2004.

Cooper, Susan Fenimore . *Rural Hours*. New York: George P. Putnam, 1850.

Deleuze, Gilles, and Félix Guattari. "Rhizome." In *Mille Plateaux: Capitalisme et schizophrénie* [A Thousand Plateaus: Capitalism and Schizophrenia]. Paris: Les Éditions de Minuit, 1980.

Dickinson, Emily. *Herbarium*. Cambridge, MA: Belknap Press of Harvard University Press, 2006.

Emerson, Ralph Waldo. *Nature*. Boston: James Munroe and Company, 1836.

Euripedes, *Alcestis*. Translated by W. Fielding Nevins. London: Longmans, Green, and Co, 1870.

Fowles, John. *The Tree.* London: Aurum Press, 1979.

Garnett, David. *Lady into Fox*. London: Chatto & Windus, 1922.

Girondo, Oliverio. "Cansancio" [Tiredness]. In *En la masmédula*. 3rd edition. Buenos Aires: Losada, 1963.

Haraway, Donna J. *Staying with the Trouble: Making Kin in the Cthulucene*. Durham, NC: Duke University Press, 2016.

Haskell, David George. *The Forest Unseen: A Year's Watch in Nature*. New York: Penguin Books, 2013.

Haskell, David George. *The Songs of Trees: Stories from Nature's Great Connectors*. New York: Viking, 2017.

Homer. *The Odyssey*. Translated by Emily Wilson. New York: W. W. Norton & Company, 2017.

Horace. "Epode II." In *The Complete Odes and Epodes.* Introduction by Betty Radice. Notes and translation by W. Shepherd. London: Penguin Classics, 1983.

Jackson, Shirley. *We Have Always Lived in the Castle*. New York: Viking, 1962.

Jiménez, Juan Ramón. "The Final Voyage." *In Esprit, Fall* 1983. Translated by Paula Luteran. Scranton: University of Scranton Department Publications, 1983.

Kafka, Franz. "Letter to Oskar Pollak, 1904." In *Letters to Friends, Family, and Editors*. Translated by Clara Winston and Richard Winston. New York: Schocken Books, 1977.

Kafka, Franz. "Wish to Become an Indian." In *Selected Stories*. Edited and translated by Mark Harman. Cambridge: Harvard University Press, 2024.

Kafka, Franz. *The Metamorphosis*. Translated by Edwin Muir and Willa Muir. New York: Schocken Books, 1972.

Lear, Linda. *Rachel Carson: Witness for Nature*. New York: Henry Holt, 1997.

León, Fray Luis de. "Secluded Life." In *The Unknown Light: The Poems of Fray Luis de León*. Translated by Willis Barnstone. Albany, NY: State University of New York Press, 1979.

Lope de Vega y Carpio, Félix. "La Filomena." In *La Filomena con otras diversas rimas, prosas y versos*. Madrid, 1621.

Machado, Antonio. "Las moscas" [The Flies]. In *Soledades, galerías y otros poemas*. Madrid: Librería Pueyo, 1907.

Maderuelo, Javier. *El espectáculo del mundo. Una historia cultural del paisaje* [The Spectacle of the World: A Cultural

History of Landscape]. Madrid: Abada, 2020.

Mancuso, Stefano. *The Incredible Journey of Plants*. New York: Other Press, 2018.

Margulis, Lynn, and Dorion Sagan. *What Is Life?*. New York: Simon and Schuster, 1995.

Monterroso, Augusto. *Movimiento perpetuo* [Perpetual Motion]. Mexico City: Joaquín Mortiz, 1972.

Neuman, Andrés. *Bariloche*. Translated by Robin Myers. Rochester: Open Letter Books, 2023.

Obligado, Clara. *La hija de Marx* [Marx's Daughter]. Barcelona: Lumen, Barcelona, 1996.

Obligado, Clara. *Si un hombre vivo te hace llorar* [If a Living Man Makes You Cry]. Barcelona: Editorial Planeta, 1999.

Obligado, Clara. *Una casa lejos de casa. La escritura extranjera* [A Home Far from Home: Foreign Writing]. Valencia: Contrabando, 2020.

Oliver, Mary. *Upstream: Selected Essays*. New York: Penguin Books, 2016.

Pasti, Umberto. *Giardini e no: Manuale di sopravvivenza botanica* [Jardines. Los verdaderos y los otros; Gardens and Not: Botanical Survival Manual]. Barcelona: Elba, 2020.

Rimbaud, Arthur. *A Season in Hell*. Translated by Donald Revell. Richmond: Omnidawn, 2007.

Rimbaud, Arthur. "Lettre à Georges lzambard, 13 mai 1871" [Letter to Georges Izambard, May 13, 1871]. *Revue européenne*, (October 1928).

Saint John of the Cross. "Dark Night of The Soul." In *The Complete Works of Saint John*. Translated by E. Allison Peers. London: Burns, Oats, & Washburn, 1953.

Saint John of the Cross. "Spiritual Canticle." In *The Complete Works of Saint John*. Translated by E. Allison Peers. London: Burns, Oats, & Washburn, 1953.

Santillana, Marquis of. "Loa de los oficios serviles" [In Praise of Humble Work]. 14th century.

Simmel, Georg. "Die Philosophie der Landschaft" [The Philosophy of Landscape]. *Sage Journals* 24, no. 7-8 (December 2007).

Solnit, Rebecca. *Wanderlust: A History of Walking*. New York: Penguin Books, 2001.

Steiner, George. "Ten (Possible) Reasons for the Sadness of Thought." *Salmagundi* 146/147 (Spring-Summer 2005): 3-32.

Steiner, George, and Cécile Ladjali. *Eloge de la transmission: Le maître et l'élève* [In Praise of Transmission]. Paris: Albin Michel, 2003.

Szymborska, Wisława. "The Three Oddest Words." In *Poems, New and Collected, 1957-1997*. Translated by Clare Cavanagh and Stanisław Baranczak. New York: Harcourt Brace International, 1998.

Tanizaki, Junichiro. *In Praise of Shadows*. Translated by Thomas J. Harper and Edward Seidensticker. Sedgwick: Leete's Island Books, 1977.

Thoreau, Henry David. *Walden: or, Life in the Woods*. Boston: Ticknor and Fields, 1854.

Zambrano, María. *Claros del bosque* [Clearings in the Forest]. Introduction by Joaquín Verdú de Gregorio. 1st reprint. Madrid: Alizana, 2020.

Zambrano, María. *La Tumba de Antígona* [Antigone's Tomb]. Mexico City: Siglo XXI, 1967.

ACKNOWLEDGMENTS

To Toni Calvo Roy, for our long friendship, for showing me the beauty of holm oaks and for introducing me to María Jesús. To Giuseppe Maio, and the Enclave Bookshop, for so many wise recommendations. To Martín Obligado, for his observations on trees and physics. To Nuria Barrios, for reminding me of a quotation from María Zambrano. To Ana Casas, for her thoughtful wisdom and observations on the self and its other self. To Irene Villarejo, for her talk on philosophy and nature. To Conchi González Catalán for her explanations about Genesis. To Javier Siedlecki, Esther Pérez, and Camila Paz for their readings and comments. To Carmen Valcárcel, for passing me a few lines of Juan Ramón Jiménez at such an appropriate moment. To Roco, as always, for almost everything.

I wrote this book in Robledillo de la Vera, Cáceres, Extremadura, Spain, between the months of October 2020 and July 2021. Lockdown and classes on Zoom allowed me to spend all four seasons there.

The original Spanish edition of this book was printed on October 4, 2021, the date on which we commemorate Francis of Assisi, patron saint of ecology, who spoke with nature and considered it to be his sister.

INTERVIEW WITH CLARA OBLIGADO BY ERICA DURANTE

Erica Durante: First of all, I'd like to ask you about the form of *all that grows: nature and writing.* It's a book comprising a sequence of fragments made up of groups of phrases, word families, and sentences that are almost lines of poetry. How did this essay take shape, and what was the seed from which it sprouted?

Clara Obligado: Over many years—and many books—I've been developing a "*mestizo* form" of writing. This doesn't allow the reader the comfort of an established genre, instead, it makes them constantly question: What kind of a book is this? It's my way of talking about foreignness, about what doesn't completely belong to one thing or another, and perhaps encourages the person reading to question the origin of genres. Being foreign through form; presenting a hybrid, impertinent text—in the sense of not belonging—is also a way of seeing the world.

ED: Reading *all that grows* from within the United States of America, both near and far from the endless horizons you describe of your childhood in the Argentinian pampa, suggests a continuity that unites the Americas from North to South, but, at the same time, your book is divided into two very distinct hemispheres. How do you conceive of geography? As something intimate, physical, or imaginary?

CO: The landscape of childhood is curious because it's simultaneously present and lost. It's lost not only because of time passing, but also because modifications to our planet and the successive erosions of climate change prevent that melancholy. My childhood landscape, lost forever, makes and shapes me. We all have landscapes within us, which witnessed our birth, and we refer to them like a mother tongue. So geography is simultaneously intimate, physical, and imaginary. It's all three things at once. From the physical point of view, I like dreaming about that great América with its line of fire to the West, tremendous volcanoes, and its line of palm trees to the East. I don't really believe in borders, I prefer to think of the planet as a whole, in motion. Wasn't South America stuck to Africa at one point? Weren't we all Pangea?

ED: *all that grows* moves effortlessly between different spaces, seasons, and climates on the planet. Your writing intuitively imitates the natural gestures that unite living organisms, transforming and recycling them. Where does your decision to link nature and writing come from? What are the limits literature comes up against in trying to reproduce the holistic being of nature?

CO: I believe we're an infinite web of meanings. Knowledge, particularly since the Enlightenment, separates and catalogs different fields in order to understand. It compartmentalizes. But each field of knowledge alone is insufficient; it needs the others. Certainly this movement of reaching outward is necessary, but so, too, is the opposite, reaching inward. Take the example of a tree; I can think of a tree and also the word "tree" that designates it, then in turn the tree can "think" of itself, doubtless in a different way, because if it couldn't "think" in some way (that is unknown to me), it wouldn't survive. The tree also holds a "written" file of its own history in the rings of its trunk. It narrates itself like an olden-day troubadour, noting down what the world around was like over the course of its life, and it's that history we can decipher. Without words I couldn't think, but doubtless other forms of thought exist that don't use words the way a writer uses them. I work at those limits of language, in that immensity, in that impossibility—in that amazement.

ED: Exile is another key intersection in your work, if not the central axis around which it turns. Expanding the form of the diary, across four decades of exile from Argentina in Spain, *all that grows* contains deep pain: the pain of the violent disappearance of a loved one by the military dictatorship, and the impossibility of saying farewell to all the others who were lost. How has this grief changed your relationship to your country? And what's it like to live with this mourning when other dictatorships are committing similar human rights abuses in Central America, South America, and other countries in the world?

CO: Experiencing a dictatorship and its violence changed me profoundly. Firstly, I became aware of the almost infinite brutality of some human beings, their cruelty. Secondly, in exile I became a foreigner, a kind of amputation. No one is born foreign, it's an identity that is branded onto you and it changes your relationship to the world. But out of that pain, the idea of the "fertile wound" germinates, an idea developed by Clarice Lispector, which brings us to a more positive vision of this experience. Having lived through all that brings me closer, without a doubt, to other situations sometimes much tougher than what I went through. It's difficult to really understand what we haven't experienced personally. Intellectually, maybe, we can understand, but not in all aspects. I'd say that pain is, among many other things, a gnosiology. Once you've lived through an experience such as mine you see everything differently. I have a very passionate relationship with my country, which I didn't have before, and I'm very sensitive to topics that previously I wasn't able to see.

ED: There are many different kinds of bodies that appear in your book: disappeared, vegetable, marine, vertebrate, invertebrate, human. There's also your own body in three distinct phases of your life: childhood, adulthood—the time of your pregnancies—and old age, your being a grandmother. It's striking to see time passing, and the way you represent your body changes dramatically. The anatomical descriptions of the child's body give way to self-portraits that are increasingly linked to the world of plants: you refer to yourself as a transplanted seed, a pregnant bulb, an aerial root, to the point of confusing yourself with all that grows. How does this change in perception come about, and where does this desire, or perhaps ontological impulse, to encompass other life forms come from?

CO: You're right, and it hadn't occurred to me. My way of thinking is gradually becoming "planetary," so to speak, inclusive. Before, I saw myself as a female human facing nature, but now I feel part of it—an increasingly small part. The pandemic made me aware of how unimportant we are. We could disappear like the dinosaurs, for example, without the planet changing much. This perception of things has come about gradually. Was I once an insect? No doubt. A fern? This is our history, we all come from something that precedes us. When I read a forest, I read myself, when I look at a root, I see my own origins. I like thinking of myself as a tiny part of evolution.

ED: As part of your increasing proximity to the vegetable world, how might you envision the possibility of narrating from a nonhuman point of view, with a nonhuman voice, taking, for example, the perspective of a tree or a root? What would that other viewpoint bring to your work?

CO: To me, it's more possible that a tree could narrate like me rather than me narrate like a tree. It's true that we are getting closer, and I have increasing respect for them. Trees amaze me. The chemistry laboratory of their roots, their whispering, and the way they exchange information in the dark. The incredible journeys they undertake, even though we think they're immobile. Their capacity to use other living beings without destroying them, their longevity. Their music and their beauty. I don't know if my language will ever get close to that of trees, but what I do know is that their stories, what I have glimpsed, are changing my way of seeing the world.

all that grows: nature and writing

First edition of 1500 published in 2025 by X Artists' Books, Los Angeles, CA
Originally published in Spanish in 2021 under the title *Todo lo que crece: Naturaleza y escritura* by Páginas de Espuma, Madrid

This publication is part of X Artists' Books' X Topics (XT) series, a collection of books focused on the writing and ideas of artists of color and other marginalized voices.

Original text by Clara Obligado
Translated by Fiona Mackintosh
Edited by Gwen Davis-Barrios, Alexandra Grant, and Nicole Hervás Ibañez
Copyedited by Poppy Coles
Proofread by Gwen Davis-Barrios, Nicole Hervás Ibañez, and Olivia Weber-Stanis
Designed by Dana Collins
Cover art by Julieta Obligado

Printed and bound by Bookmobile
Typeset in Filosofia, Mr Eaves San OT book, and Mr Eaves San OT book italic.
Printed on 12 pt C1S White stock with matte softtouch lamination (cover) and 60# Boise offset white (pages).

Library of Congress Control Number: 2025930712
ISBN: 9798990698512

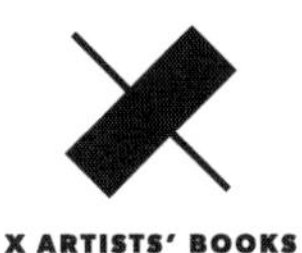

X ARTISTS' BOOKS